THE NEXT BREATH

NEW LIFE AFTER NEAR DEATH

Joseph Fisher, Ph.D., M.P.H.
www.the-next-breath.org

Copyright 2015 © Joseph Fisher
Joe Fisher Books
PO Box 129
Sanibel, FL 33957
www.the-next-breath.org

Cover design by Christopher Fous
Interior formatting by Veronica Yager

ISBN: 978-09905678-2-0

SYNOPSIS

CHAPTER ONE: A SURVIVOR'S TALE

Describes the immediate medical emergency, the author's reaction to it, and the barriers to seeking treatment and diagnosis.

CHAPTER TWO: HOSPITALIZATION

Discusses the introduction and immersion of a patient into the hospital routine, a chaotic world of diffused responsibility, information overload and the need to evaluate treatment options and ways to obtain the "best" treatment in that context.

CHAPTER THREE: THE NEW NORMAL— PTSD AND BEYOND

Considers the physical and psychological adaptation to the life threatening experience, symptoms of Post-Traumatic Stress Disorder (PTSD), medical treatment and self-help.

CHAPTER FOUR: VICTIMIZATION—FATE AND FORGIVENESS

Examines the origins of depression following a life threatening event – answering the question *Why Me?*; the need to find a cause, place blame, find fault and bring those responsible to account; and gaining wisdom through self-understanding and freedom from depression through forgiveness.

CHAPTER FIVE: FACING OBLIVION

Discusses the implications of the sudden and stark confrontation with death, mortality and oblivion and considers the questions: *What's God got to do with it? Where will I find peace?*

CHAPTER SIX: WINNOWING—
THE WINDOW OF OPPORTUNITY

Explores the process of simplifying one's life by deciding what is important, a process that includes answering questions such as, *Who do I love? What do I want to do with my remaining time?*

CHAPTER SEVEN: RELAPSE

Describes additional life threatening events experienced by the author – a near fatal Coumadin-related bleed out and consequent deep vein thromboses and pulmonary embolism – and considers these events in the context of modern medical decision-making.

CHAPTER EIGHT: EPILOGUE

Summarizes the insights gained from being brought back from the edge of death and experiencing a new life event.

For:

> *Dorit – Life Partner – who loved me back to life.*
>
> *Jake – Sentimental stoic – the bravest person I know.*
>
> *Jane – Quiet leader – the calm in the storm.*

On the death of his child:

Dew evaporates

and all our world is dew...

so dear, so fresh, so fleeting

Kobayashi Issa
(1763 - 1828)

CONTENTS

INTRODUCTION   1

CHAPTER ONE: A SURVIVOR'S TALE   7

The Crisis   8

Seeking Treatment   13

Diagnosis: Pulmonary Embolism   19

Epilogue   24

CHAPTER TWO: HOSPITALIZATION   31

Hospitalists   34

Coumadin   41

**CHAPTER THREE: THE NEW NORMAL— PTSD
AND TREATMENT**   55

PTSD   57

Prevalence   58

Brain Imaging   60

Manifestations   62

Superstitious Behavior   67

Summary   70

TREATMENT AND RECOVERY   71

The Circle of Life   71

The Pharmacalization of Society   73

Mantras and Meditation   78

Getting Better   83

CHAPTER FOUR: VICTIMIZATION—FATE AND FORGIVENESS   **85**

Mistakes   65

Malpractice   67

Professional Forgiveness   97

Personal Forgiveness   101

The Power of Apology   104

Epilogue   108

Chapter Five: Facing Oblivion   **111**

Miracles   115

The Power of Prayer   119

Tent Revival   124

Death andmmortality   127

NDE's   134

An Agnostic Doubts   138

CHAPTER SIX: WINNOWING—SHEDDING AND LEAVING BEHIND   **141**

Hitting Bottom   145

Death and Dying vs. Life and Living   148

Relationships   155

Finding Purpose   162

CHAPTER SEVEN: RELAPSE   **169**

Bleeding to Death   170

Therapeutic Dilemmas   185

Pondering Imponderables   193

CHAPTER EIGHT: EPILOGUE—STARTING OVER   **195**

NOTES   **205**

Chapter One: A Survivor's Tale   205

Chapter Two: Hospitalization   207

Chapter Three: The New Normal – PTSD
and Treatment   212

Chapter Four: Victimization – Fate
and Forgiveness   216

Chapter Five: Facing Oblivion   216

Chapter Six: Winnowing – Shedding
and Leaving Behind   219

Chapter Seven: Relapse   220

ACKNOWLEDGEMENTS   **221**

ABOUT THE AUTHOR   **223**

INTRODUCTION

What is it like to be suddenly, catastrophically on the verge of death? While it is something few of us actually experience, we all probably entertain the thought at some time. But no amount of anticipatory visualization of what one might do under the circumstance can fully prepare a person for that moment. No amount of contemplation of how one will be affected afterward can capture how indelibly it etches the psyche. It is a moment when clarity reigns and nothing will ever be the same.

For me that time came as I was walking on the beach, ironically trying to get in shape for a planned trek to the Himalayas. A chronic and massive deep vein thrombosis (DVT) spawned an equally massive pulmonary embolism (PE) that lodged in my pulmonary arteries in the process totally incapacitating my right lung. In the time it took to take a single step I crossed a threshold passing from apparent excellent health to being mortally wounded — desperately choking, gasping to breathe — my life suspended by a thin thread of chance.

At that moment, one is very much in the moment, trying to find answers to very basic questions: *What went wrong? How bad is it? How can I get help?* Most importantly: *Will I die?* Medical explanations lose all meaning at a time like that. The chance of dying, over 50% in my case as best I can assess my chances in retrospect, is completely irrelevant. For the person in the moment the odds are much simpler. It is either 1 or 0, you either die or you don't.

Getting help "in time" means very little either. One is balanced on the keen edge of fate. Help arrives when it does and by then a cascade of contingencies has already decided for or against the stricken. The immediate denouement comes when one enters the safe harbor of professional medical care and one surrenders their well-being to its authority. There are few things modern medicine does with regularity that are quite as inspirational as saving the near dead.

Although physical recovery after the crisis can be remarkably rapid, repair of the psyche can take far longer. The stricken person survived a potentially life ending event. They were transported suddenly to the threshold of oblivion, stripped of all defense and artifice and forced to confront nonexistence and mortality without time to prepare.

While dying and near death experiences have been studied for some time, this is a qualitatively different experience as is the psychological recovery process. What has happened is best conceptualized as a **sudden life event**. The patient is adapting less to the prospect of death than to the prospect of living with a new perception of existence with all the portent and potential that implies.

Near death experiences meanwhile with common reports of out-of-body sensations, bright tunnels, feelings of calm, spectral personages in white garments and so forth may shed light on the process of dying, but not on adjustment to life after a brush with sudden death. Adjustment to a sudden life event is not unlike the process of grieving before death outlined by Elisabeth Kübler-Ross. Both have stages of adaptation as well as commonalities among psychological reactions. But one is forward looking while the other involves coming to terms with the past.

Certainly Post-Traumatic Stress Disorder (PTSD) describes some of what is going on. Preoccupation with the event, repeatedly revisiting it, hyper-vigilance to bodily signs that might presage another event, phobias of the place where it occurred, depressive symptoms such as failure to complete tasks, inability to plan, lack of energy and so forth were feelings I experienced and still do occasionally.

But there is more. Among the most immediate and prominent feeling I can recall is the sense of being singled out unfairly, of being a victim, and having a need to blame someone for my predicament. Regardless, of the objective basis for the feelings, they are common among survivors, very real and at worst self-defeating, tending to exacerbate the ever-present depression. Only through forgiveness of my caretakers and myself was I able to free myself of the burdens of blaming.

Threatening our existence as they do, sudden life threatening events bring us abruptly into direct confrontation with the self-annihilating truth of our own mortality and the shared mystery of all existence—what happens after. Under the circumstances even the most agnostic among us, a group in which I number myself, often recognize the supernatural as the most plausible reason they still live. Whether one gives credence to this type of causality or not, a person is more apt to entertain spiritual explanations for their continued existence for having balanced on the cusp of the alternative.

Looking back with the clarity of what might have been, few matters appear as important as they did at the time. The recognition of the inherent silliness, for lack of a better term, of where I once chose to expend my energies combined with the knowledge of how tenuous existence is, set off a period of intense introspection, a wholesale search to answer the question: Who and what is important to me? The attempt to identify what matters, to winnow the possibilities to the essentials can be transformative as life veers in new directions.

Above all else running headlong into the wall of one's own mortality and escaping to continue living can be the impetus for a profoundly moving period of self-examination and change. I have never loved my wife and family with such intensity as after. Despite my best efforts to man up and suppress my emotions, I wept out of gratitude as I tried to thank those who loved me, not only for the obligatory care and comfort they provide as necessary and nourishing as it was, but because they loved and accepted me as I was and wept along with me.

Personal vulnerability, both physical and emotional, dominated in the period immediately following the accident. All my defenses, the carefully constructed bulwarks against unfiltered and embarrassing emotions were stripped from me. Patterns of interactions and the web of relationships that define everyday life were cut loose from their anchors. This window of opportunity for change was to be fleeting and short-lived. But while it lasted it proved to be a chance to take a Mulligan on life. One of the rare times we have the insight and need not just to rewind the tape and pick up where we left off but to push the reset button and start life anew.

What follows then is a description of one person's near fatal medical emergencies and life rebuilding recovery. It is an idiosyncratic journey and I do not pretend the psychological after effects I report occur in a set order of stages or for that matter will be universally observed by everyone who has a similar crisis. Nor do I suggest my medical emergency, a pulmonary embolism, and recovery from it can be equated exactly with other sudden mortality-facing experiences such as combat or heart attacks. Each of these has its own unique situational features that give it a character all its own.

At the core, I believe (and numerous blog posts would seem to support my view) this process of healing and adaptation is common to all who have confronted death in an unexpected moment regardless of the proximate cause. I suspect my fellow survivors may not have every reaction I did or give them the same significance I do. Nor will they use the same language to describe what they went through. Nevertheless, I think they will recognize my journey as a road they traveled too. They will have their own stories and anecdotes to mark the milestones along the way and express the life-affirming process they have undergone and the context within which it took place.

A final note. Everything described in this book, no matter how coincidental or seemingly apocryphal, did in fact happen. There is indeed a Dr. Badov and he was assigned to my care at one point. A stranger did confront me on a deserted beach with a question for the ages. My former wife did emerge from three decades of silence to tell me she was dying just as I was contemplating my own mortality. I have tried to recount each of these instances and the other events, thoughts, feeling and emotions that accompanied or were caused by my narrow escape from death as accurately as I can recall them. The fact that the unusual often occurred with apparent literary serendipity to flesh out the story just proves, I suppose, that you can never hope to make up the best stuff.

Joe Fisher, 2015

CHAPTER ONE
A SURVIVOR'S TALE

"Life is what happens to you while you're busy
making other plans."

—*John Lennon*
(1940 - 1980)

It was the first day of spring and I felt great. For months I had been bothered by persistent pain in my left leg. It was red, hot to the touch, sore and slightly swollen, all indications of restricted blood flow. I had been plagued too for weeks with a general malaise. I just didn't feel well, although I could point to no one specific reason or constellation of symptoms that would explain this unease. It seemed to manifest itself most often as night sweats, waking me in the first black hours of the day to find my pillow and bedclothes drenched in perspiration.

But today I felt great. The day before I swam a mile and was experiencing no ill effects. Most importantly there was no pain in my lower leg. So today it was time to start training for my next trek. This was to be my third trip to the Himalayas, a planned three-week, cross-country odyssey from Kathmandu in Nepal to remote western Tibet. The goal was to be at Mt. Kailash, a peak reputed to be the home of Vishnu and sacred to one quarter of the world's population, in time for the Saga Dawa festival in early May. There I would join other pilgrims in a ritual circumnavigation of the mountain at altitudes of 18,500 ft., a journey said to cleanse one of a lifetime of sin upon completion. I toyed with the notion of doing two laps just to be sure.

Here it was already mid-March and I needed to get in some semblance of fitness if I were to have a chance of making the circuit. Lose 20 pounds, well maybe more, and since my excursions to the Himalayas did not involve climbing high peaks, but rather hiking long distances at high altitudes, it meant toughening my feet and legs in preparation. So I began my pre-trek regimen of dieting and long walks along the beach near my home on Sanibel Island, Florida. As helpful as walking at sea level was it could not possibly prepare me adequately for three weeks of walking in the rarified air above 14,000 feet. But I had to start somewhere.

The Crisis

So off I went to the beach and started to hike along the shore. It was a glorious morning, warm and brilliant. The not yet fully ascendant sun bathed the beach in a candescent glow and reflected off the dappled water to create dancing flashes of light. I was pain free, so out of the ordinary I took notice. It would be an exceptional day, I was sure.

Then a quarter of a mile from the beach access, less than ten minutes into the hike I was starting to hit stride when I took a single step and in that span I went from being healthy, vigorous and in good shape, to a person on the edge of death whose odds of surviving the next five minutes might be no better than two to one against. In that one stride my life changed irrevocably.

I was immediately aware that something had gone terribly wrong. But it was the second step that confirmed something catastrophic had occurred. From my sternum to my spine, under my arm to the end of my ribcage the entire right side of my body was constricted as if clamped in place. It was as if a malevolent giant had placed the heel of one hand on my breastbone and the other on my backbone, linked fingers under my armpit and held fast.

My chest would not move, it would not inflate. It was not so much painful as it was a constriction. I could not take in air. Somehow I felt the condition was transitory and would abate with the next intake, but it did not. I was gasping for breath, air coming into my starved lungs as raspy gulps.

I took halting steps away from the water, moving toward the dunes not more than 10 yards away. My heart was racing, my pulse palpitating and irregular. Despite the ambient temperature above 90 degrees I was instantly cold and clammy. And oh, the anxiety. I needed to run, to flee, but unable to do so and not knowing where to go in any case.

In the dunes, half hidden among the sea oats and saw grass I spied a beach chair stashed there for future use. Its allure was overpowering, beckoning me with the promise of relief. For a moment I wanted nothing more than to sit, to rest and wait for my body to return to normal. Somehow though I knew intuitively and without a scintilla of doubt that if sat I would never rise again.

I grabbed my cell phone, my lifeline, and called my wife as much to end my isolation as to get help. Between huge gulps for air I was able to blurt out "I can't breathe. I don't know what's wrong. I just can't breathe." My gasping was so extreme, my sister, who was traveling with my wife at the time, could hear it across the car even though the receiver was pressed against my wife's ear. She asked me where I was and promised to come immediately to pick me up.

I paced in small circles waiting, heart racing, anxious and oxygen starved. Although I was vaguely aware I was on the verge of death there was no real terror associated with that possibility. I was much too preoccupied with the immediate here and now of the event. My mental state was characterized by hypersensitivity to my body, ever vigilant for signs that would signal what would transpire next. I had no time to worry about death and nonexistence or the finality of separation from loved ones that implied. All that would come but much later.

As minutes passed my heartbeat slowed and the anxiety slackened enough for me to take stock of my condition. There were only two explanations for what was happening. I was either having a heart attack or I just had a pulmonary embolism, a blood clot that forms in an extremity, pieces of which can break off, travel through the heart to the lungs cutting off its blood supply. Anxiety, heart palpitations, breathing difficulties, feeling cold and clammy are symptoms of each, I knew.

Controlling my anxiety marginally, I performed a quick self-triage. The constriction was on my right side only. There was little real pain, just the suffocating constriction. By comparison, my left side was completely uninvolved, a fact I would later find out saved my life. More importantly, I had none of the crushing pain in the middle of my chest, like an elephant sitting on it as it is often described by heart attack survivors. There were no shooting pains in my left arm. Other symptoms, erratic heartbeat, difficulty breathing did not differentiate. I just had a pulmonary embolism (PE) I concluded.

On a personal level I was not unfamiliar with PEs. My mother had, in fact, died of a massive one some years before. She had been stricken and stood over a bathroom sink gazing incredulous at herself in the mirror before slumping to the floor, her pallor turning ever more gray, until she perished from asphyxiation. Or so it was recounted by my sister who was with her at the time of her death; ironically the same sister who was in the car when my wife received my first desperate call.

The story of my mother's death impressed me indelibly. The suddenness of her demise frightened me the most. The finality of it. So quick that no help could be summoned and reach her no matter how consequential it might have proven to be. No time to say goodbye, to have last words with loved ones. After her death PEs were a morbid phobia of mine and I was hyper-vigilant for signs that could indicate I might have one. And yet here I was reliving my mother's dying moments.

But as the minutes passed, it became increasingly clear I would not succumb immediately. My breathing, albeit labored, became less desperate as my now rested body required less oxygen. My heartbeat slowed and became regular as my anxiety diminished. The immediate crisis was over. Maybe it wasn't so bad after all. With that thought stupidity took over. At that moment I was quite literally one half inch from dying where I stood, the size of a second embolism that would have stopped my heart. Yet, even though I was certain of what had just happened and I suspected the gravity of my situation my reaction was equal parts denial, procrastination and magical thinking.

The next precious minutes were spent arguing with myself about what to do. My mother died of a pulmonary embolism in less than 15 minutes. I was still alive and ambulatory, so I would not succumb I reasoned. Perhaps I overreacted. Maybe it wasn't as serious as I thought. Feeling somewhat abashed that I might have overplayed the incident I called my wife to let her know the crisis was over and that I would walk home. I also took the opportunity to point out that breathing was still a challenge so she would not interpret my first call as a hypochrondriacal figment of an overactive imagination.

I did not so much walk home as proceed with a shuffling trudge. I lacked the energy to lift my foot in order to take a step. Instead I dragged my feet along the shell road raising a small cloud of silicon dust around my shoes. All the while I struggled to breathe by drawing air through my clenched teeth. The constriction in my side was painful now. Breathing through the pain, my lips drew back over my teeth in a sardonic grin as I braced against the tightness.

Plodding along I retraced my route from the beach to my house two blocks away. Lingering in the back of my mind was the pregnant question: What should I do now that the crisis was past? Should I go immediately to the hospital? Should I wait at home to determine the trajectory of the problem, whether it would improve or worsen?

It was Saturday. Spending hours in an emergency room waiting to be seen, only to find it was not as serious as I supposed was a prospect I was not willing to entertain. The contrary possibility, that I needed immediate hospitalization for a life threatening condition, did not rise to the level of consideration. The threat simply did not seem real or immediate enough, since by virtue of my mother's example I deemed myself in no danger of imminent death. I decided to wait until Monday when I could see my personal physician and let him decide the appropriate course of action.

Doubts still lingered, however, about the course of action I had chosen. My sister lobbied hard for me to seek attention. She told my wife in confidence, "I have seen this before. He needs to go to the hospital immediately." But I obstinately held to the belief that I could delay. If I were to change my mind I would need incontrovertible evidence that I needed to seek medical care before I would go. To prove to myself this was not the case I devised tests, physical challenges designed to provoke a worsening of my condition, deliberately tempting fate to prove to myself I was all right. One such occurred immediately upon arriving home when I decided to sweep out the garage, despite the exertion and dust raised exacerbating my breathing.

I have often marveled in retrospect about my foolhardy stubbornness. Was it an integral part of my personality, the need to take care of myself, to make my own decisions, to require proof? Or was my reaction in some way a consequence of the event and its psychological sequalae? Was denial a more universal response than mine alone, springing perhaps from a common desire to diminish the gravity of one's condition? Did most people procrastinate before seeking help? Did they create implausible reasons to persuade themselves that they did not need treatment?

In my case certainly the potential for embarrassment played a role. I had a reputation, perhaps well-earned, among my family as being something of a hypochondriac. To go to the hospital in an ambulance outside of normal hours only to find out that nothing was too seriously wrong had personal and psychic costs for me. It is difficult with hindsight to understand how the fear of making a fool of myself could trump the fear of suddenly dying from a preventable cause, but it did. By that point though, I was already visualizing the future after diagnosis not evaluating the present danger. This behavior became all the more baffling when I learned that even another small embolism could have ended my life during these days of delay.

Seeking Treatment

Whatever the reason for my behavior, the next two days were spent living in the delusion of my own making. The medical signs were obvious. Walking up a flight of stairs caused me to double over at the waist gasping for breath as badly as I had on the beach. I dreaded climbing the second flight of stairs to go to bed each night and the gasping and emptiness in my chest that waited at the top.

I dreaded too the black loneliness of night that waited there when I was alone with my thoughts and fears. Lying still while I repeatedly scanned my body for sensory signs that I was all right or not. Rolling over in my mind the events of the day, the decisions made or not made and the possibility that I chose in error. Wondering about the small divergences in life's path and their consequences that I could never hope to foresee at the time. Always searching for the answer: would I live until morning?

I tried to keep up a semblance of normalcy through the weekend. It proved to be impossible. I was worn out, weak and preoccupied with my fears and questions. The very act of breathing became an arduous relay. Forcing my ribs to expand to fill my damaged lung yet never feeling as if enough was air taken in. Deeply inhaling but always coming up short. Trying to pull harder but never getting more. The process had to be repeated every few seconds. It was tedious, exhausting and without relief.

Monday finally came. I was able to see my primary care physician in the afternoon. As I sat panting in the examination room, he checked my respiration and measured the oxygen saturation in my blood. Air was moving in and out of my lungs unobstructed, while my blood oxygen level stood at 97%, both quite normal. Whatever was causing my respiratory distress it was not preventing life-sustaining oxygenation of tissues and organs throughout my body. Discounting my obvious respiratory distress in the face of the results, the doctor saw no reason for me to go to the hospital immediately. I enjoyed a brief moment of smug self-satisfaction when he seemed to confirm that I had made the right decision not to rush to the emergency room over the weekend.

Instead, he ordered an ultrasound test of my legs two days hence to rule out the presence of blood clots in my lower extremities. These clots or deep vein thromboses (DVTs) are the chief source of pulmonary emboli if that were the cause of my symptoms. On the way out of his office the nurse supervisor wished me luck, a sentiment I found odd until eventually I learned that luck had everything to do with my survival.

Ultrasounds are benign diagnostic tests, noninvasive ones since they require no penetration of the body. Instead ultrasound waves emitted by a wand bounce off the underlying structures and are read as they return, showing the contours of what lies beneath, in effect sonar for examining the underlying body topography.

Ultrasound scans are particularly useful in visualizing soft tissues such as veins and hence are an excellent tool for discovering the presence of a blood clot. In this case, the wand is passed along the vein in question. At intervals it is pressed down by the technician. If the vein compresses, that is, one wall of the vein can be forced to touch the opposite side, it is clear of any obstruction. If on the other hand it does not compress, a blood clot is indicated.

I arrived at the testing facility almost exactly four days after the original accident full of expectation for a final determination of what had happened. No stranger to ultrasounds I was calm and at ease. Given my family history of PE's I had occasion to have several over the preceding years. I lay relaxed while the technician efficiently scanned my right leg. Moving to the left leg she repeated the procedure.

Upon completion she said demurely, "Would you mind taking a seat in the waiting room while I call your physician?" But while this should have sounded ominous were I not in such deep denial, it brought on a sense of relief instead since I would soon have a definitive answer as to what, if anything, ailed me. A few minutes later she poked her head out of the examination room. "Your doctor would like you to go to the emergency room right away," she said.

The ultrasound report, obtained much later, details the extent of the thromboses and hence the cause for alarm.

————

Noninvasive Vascular Report

Indications:

> Dyspnea (shortness of breath) and edema (swelling)

History:

> Patient states onset of shortness of breath x 4 days (4 days ago). Left leg swelling. Patient denies right leg symptoms.
>
> Venous exam 12/2009 revealed negative for DVT and venous insufficiency.

Findings:

> Rt. Lower Venous: Chronic wall changes of right peripheral vein. The remaining visualized veins appear patent at this time.
>
> Lt. Lower Venous: Positive for acute deep vein thrombosis of the distal femoral/proximal popliteal vein (abductor level), popliteal and posterior tibial veins. The peroneal veins were not identified. The remaining veins appear patent.

Conclusions:

> Positive for acute deep vein thrombosis of the
> left lower extremity.

Comments:

> Verbal preliminary report given by the sonographer.

> Patient sent to ER

———

While the right leg did evidence venous deficiencies there was no evidence of clots, i.e., the veins were "patent". By comparison, the left leg had extensive DVT's. Of most concern were the clots in the popliteal vein which runs behind the knee and up the thigh. Clots above the knee are especially prone to throw off pieces and spawn pulmonary emboli. The clots in the lower leg and calf, the tibial and peroneal veins respectively, while troublesome are less likely to have pieces separate.

The ultrasound did not conclusively show that I had experienced a PE, but it did provide a high degree of suspicion that one had occurred. Even if not, blood clots in the leg of the extent and magnitude observed are health risks in their own right and demand immediate medical attention.

Upon hearing my doctor's directive to go immediately to the ER all my illusions of good health and unassisted recovery were shattered. The defenses I so carefully constructed collapsed. A crystalline reality shown through – I was in grave danger. The possibility of dying was suddenly very real again. I felt the overwhelming need to communicate with loved ones, to say goodbye, to leave an expression of what they meant to me and what I hoped for them should I not be there to watch their lives unfold or communicate with them again. So I hastily sent text messages to my wife and two young adult children.

This action gave me some respite against the rush of time. Although I derived some comfort from the realization that I would soon be safe, under care and in a setting where treatment resources could be marshaled if needed, a tyranny of urgency took over. The person who had responded to a major medical crisis with aggressive nonchalance and perilous procrastination, now fretted that another devastating event would occur before reaching the emergency room, a trip of no more than five minutes. All the worry about suspicious symptoms that had been denied, diminished or blocked from consciousness before flared anew in response to the confirmation they were indeed real.

Fortunately the ER was immediately across the street. I drove there and walked into the waiting room. Then began a drama that can only be created by the way modern medical care is delivered in America. I had just passed into the Medico-Pharma Twilight Zone. Only the sonorous voiceover of Rod Serling was missing.

I went to the receptionist, told her who I was, where I had come from and assured her my physician called ahead to vouch for the fact that I needed immediate care. I was referred instead to the billing area where I was required to provide evidence of my financial bona fides. Having completed that task I returned to the receptionist and informed her that no administrative barrier remained to prevent me from seeing a physician. Unimpressed she told me to take a seat until I was called.

Two hours went by. The waiting room emptied, filled and emptied again. Finally, my sense of fair play got the better of me. My turn should have come up long before. So I returned to the receptionist ready to demand to see a physician and unwilling to take no for an answer this time. The hypocrisy of petulantly demanding treatment after having avoided it for days never occurred to me. This was a matter of principle after all. I plead my case pointing out that the need for emergency care was a directive of my primary care physician who obviously believed I was in mortal danger. She was nonplussed and cooled me out by saying I would be next.

I returned to my chair in the waiting room. Fifteen minutes later I was finally called and ushered in to see a triage nurse. Total elapsed time since arrival: 2 hours and 45 minutes. This being a weekday morning with a full complement of physicians and nurses on duty, I could only imagine what the wait would have been had I come in on the weekend.

Through the halting breaths I gave the triage nurse a history of the accident, physician visit and ultrasound results. To my astonishment the nurse ignored the information given and asked, "How did you get here?"

"I drove," I replied.

"Did someone drive you?"

"No, I drove myself."

"Why did you drive yourself?"

"Because I was told by my doctor to come to the ER immediately," I said, assuming this was obvious.

"No," she scolded. "Why didn't you call an ambulance?"

I was incredulous. "Because I was just across the street," I exclaimed.

Having reached the end of the interrogation she launched into a lecture. "There are some people who come to the ER in an ambulance who shouldn't," she opined. "There are some people who do not come by ambulance but should," she continued and concluded. "You are one of those".

I agreed she had a point even though it seemed quite irrelevant since I was there and ready for treatment. Besides I was only a quarter of a mile away, I pointed out one more time. She was unmoved. It was also clear she had no intention of letting me proceed until I at last repented. Recognizing I was without leverage in this debate, I fervently said I would never again, if faced with the same situation, drive myself to the emergency room. This promise of respect for protocol seemed to placate her but not enough to prevent her from sending me back to the waiting room, perhaps to contemplate my misbehavior. Ten more minutes passed before I was called to see a physician.

In retrospect I often wondered about this exchange. Was it a juvenile exercise of power by an authority-obsessed gatekeeper? Was it a testament to the monumental inefficiency of the typical emergency room and the callous disregard of the staff? Or was it something structural in the way emergency rooms are organized and deliver care? Perhaps an ambulance is a symbolic indicator that the occupant needs immediate treatment, the golden passkey that can cut through any bureaucratic barriers. After all the ambulance delivers patients to a separate entrance, disgorging passengers directly into the ER, bypassing the process of payment proof and treatment prioritization.

An ambulance has symbolic significance for the patient as well. It is an admission that they feel their condition is an emergency and requires care as quickly as it can be delivered. In my pre-diagnosis mental state, I was not prepared to make that concession. But I was capable of learning. Whatever the role and meaning of an ambulance in determining the need for care, when presented with the same choice, ride or drive, again a few months later, I chose to ride.

Diagnosis: Pulmonary Embolism

Once ushered inside, the emergency room was a model of efficiency. Within minutes, I gave a history, vital signs were taken, and I was transported to radiology to get a CT scan of my lungs. Shortly after the ER physician came in to deliver the verdict. My condition was in fact caused by a very large blood clot, a massive pulmonary embolism, that blocked all the arteries to my right lung.

A clot is often confused with or considered to be synonymous with a scab but the two differ in several important ways. A scab is a hard crust that seals a wound, re-establishing body integrity and protecting it from external hazards. A clot by comparison stops blood flow at the site of a wound. It can be a necessary precursor to the formation of a scab since scabs cannot form in the presence of flowing blood. However a clot, known medically as a thrombosis, bears little physical resemblance to a scab. It is instead a gelatinous mass that is soft, flexible and malleable. Its flexibility allows it to conform to the contours of the space around the wound while its size and heft make it difficult to displace by the backpressure of flowing blood.

But clots can move if the pressure is too great and once dislodged they move freely through the body or out of it. Freed of its mooring, a clot is called an embolism. Clots that originate in leg veins, so-called deep vein thrombosis or DVT's, once dislodged will move effortlessly with the blood to the heart, aided by their soft shape-shifting features. A journey that is further enabled by the fact that travel through the veins becomes easier as the clot nears the heart since the veins increase in size and diameter along the way.

Entering the heart, the clot arrives in the collection point, the right atrium chamber where it subsequently flows into the right ventricle. The ventricle in turn pumps the oxygen-depleted blood through the pulmonary arteries to the lungs where it will be reoxygenated. The newly enriched blood is returned to the left side of the heart through the pulmonary veins. It collects again in the atrium, flows to the left ventricle and is dispersed to waiting tissues and organs throughout the body, thereby completing the oxygenating portion of the circulation system.

Mobile clots, emboli, have characteristics that make them pathologically able to disrupt this process with life-ending consequences. Clots travel to and through the heart painlessly without betraying their movement. Lack of sensory nerves in the veins and heart make an embolus undetectable until it reaches a stopping point and disrupts a body function. It is only when the clot goes into the pulmonary artery and can go no further creating a blockage that interferes with blood flow and oxygen exchange that it becomes noticeable therefore.

The pulmonary artery branches into three main divisions, each bringing oxygen- depleted blood to a lobe of the lung, named without creativity, the upper, middle, and lower lobes. Arterial branching continues as the circulatory network approaches the site of oxygen exchange, the air sacs or alveoli. The alveoli are surrounded by a mass of capillaries some that carry oxygen impoverished blood from the heart and others that, after oxygen exchange, will return oxygenated or oxygen rich blood to the left side of the heart. PEs disrupt this process by blocking the pulmonary arteries before the blood can reach the alveoli and can be rejuvenated.

The plastic nature of the clot allows it to branch with the vein and travel as far along the branching process as room allows. Therein lies the fatal potential of the pulmonary embolism. If the clot is relatively small it will travel to the smaller branches of the pulmonary veins, disrupting blood flow and the reoxygenation process only slightly. Clots of this sort may cause little, limited or unrecognizable changes in circulation or respiration. In fact, PE's may be much more common than thought because a substantial number exists below the threshold of serious damage and awareness.

However, as the size of the clot increases, so does the capacity to cause pernicious changes. The clot can block the pulmonary artery to a single lobe of a lung creating noticeable constriction and diminished respiratory capacity. Bigger still and it can affect multiple lobes and in the worst cases, both lungs. If the clots restrict respiration significantly the victim can slowly asphyxiate, dying from a lack of oxygen in a few minutes to a quarter of an hour as my mother did.

Ultimately though, a pulmonary embolism is a cardiac problem not a pulmonary one. If the clot is sufficiently large it will stop the flow of blood entirely in which case death is nearly instantaneous. The heart cannot pump blood beyond the clot, it stops beating, and the victim loses consciousness and dies.

If the patient survives the lungs are often damaged sometimes beyond repair. Below the clot, away from the heart, the alveoli collapse due to lack of oxygen caused by restricted respiratory capacity, a process known as atelectasis. Atelectasis can cause permanent changes over time if the cause is chronic e.g. from Chronic Obstructive Pulmonary Disease (COPD). But in the case of an acute cause such as a pulmonary embolism the alveoli will most often reinflate when normal airflow is restored.

With respect to cardiac changes, blood can be restricted to parts of the lung itself causing an infraction or death of the tissue nourished by the affected arteries. This is analogous to a myocardial infarction or heart attack where portions of the heart muscle die due to a clot in the coronary arteries causing a stoppage of blood flow to a section of the heart. The pulmonary embolism can cause a similar localized death, infarction, of lung tissue. Unlike atelectasis however damage from an infraction is permanent.

A better sense of the process and the damage caused is shown by it the following selected excerpts from the CT scan results that confirmed the presence of a massive PE when I was stricken on the beach.

———

Examination: CTA Chest

Clinical History:

Possible Pulmonary Embolus

Results:

There is a large embolus in the right main pulmonary artery that extends into the right upper lobe, right middle lobe and right lower lobe. There is some contrast that flows around the margin of the embolus.

The left-sided pulmonary vessels are patent.

Bone window images demonstrate dependent atelectasis.

There is some scarring in the right apex.

Impression:

1. Large right pulmonary embolus

2. Dependent atelectasis.

The effect of the plasticity of the clot can be visualized by the description in the report. The clot involved the entire right lung branching with the pulmonary artery and shutting off blood flow in all three lobes of the right lung. In effect, the right lung ceased to operate. Below the clot the lung had collapsed (dependent atelectasis) and there was evidence of pulmonary infarction (scarring in the right apex-or upper portion of the right lung). Meanwhile the left lung was uninvolved, all "vessels were patent" i.e. free from clots.

This report could be the definitional equivalent of a near miss. After the fact a pulmonologist commented that had the clot been perhaps just a centimeter larger, four-tenths of an inch, I would have died on the beach. The difference between life and death was less than half an inch. It was a sobering thought from which a cascade of emotional and behavioral consequences flowed for the next two years.

The report too provides some suggestions for my good fortune. First, consistent with my symptoms, the left lung was not involved at all explaining the ribcage constriction on the right side only. Second, there are hints that total circulatory function in the right lung was not shut down entirely. The observation that "some contrast that flows around the margins of the embolus" suggests that the clots did not completely occlude the pulmonary arteries but rather allowed some blood to flow around the sides. On such small margins life or death is decided.

Armed with a definitive diagnosis the ER staff swung into action. An IV was put in my arm and an anticoagulant (Lovenox – low molecular weight heparin) was injected into my lower abdomen to prevent any further formation of blood clots and pulmonary emboli. Having performed its function to diagnose and stabilize, the ER staff made arrangements to pass responsibility for my continued care to the adjoining hospital where I was transported and admitted.

At that point I relaxed, almost deflated as all the muscles released and I seemed to sink into the mattress. Only then did I realize how rigidly I had been holding myself. But I knew. At last, I knew. My beachfront diagnosis was confirmed I was not exaggerating. I needed to be there. The problem had a name and now it could be treated. I was on the road to recovery and I had nothing more to worry about. Or so I thought.

Epilogue

Some months after the attack I decided to begin a memoir of my experience. I thought it might be informative to get the reactions of other people who were present or were directly affected by the events. So I asked those with first-hand knowledge, my wife, daughter and sister to write a short description of how they were affected – their observations, thoughts, fears during those fateful four days. The only person who complied with this request was my sister Ellen. It was perhaps too raw and frightening for the others.

As mentioned previously, my sister was visiting the day I had the PE and she remained throughout the crisis before I was hospitalized and treatment began. She was also present at my mother's death from a pulmonary embolism two decades earlier. As a consequence, Ellen had a unique perspective from which to observe and to provide an eyewitness account of my wife and my response to the crisis and the events that transpired while matters were very much in doubt.

Her description (following) in many ways confirms my own recollections[1] while providing greater depth that could only come from an interested and familiar outsider.

> The clerk was slowly sliding my few purchases through the scanning device. Bailey's on Sanibel Island, is an institution. I was there with my sister-in-law, Dorit,

---

[1] Discrepancies in my and my sister's recall of events are discussed in Chapter 1 Notes.

picking up a few items that I wanted to contribute to the household during my visit. I felt as sleepy and relaxed as the clerk until I was suddenly – and dramatically – lifted out of my trance by Dorit.

"Put them all down, NOW!" she was yelling as she grabbed my arm and moved me toward the door. "We have to go!"

I looked at the clerk. He was a young guy and he was clearly as confused by this demanding behavior as I was.

Embarrassed and apologetic, I mumbled "sorry" and followed Dorit out to the car. She was clearly agitated as she explained to me that Joe (her husband and my younger brother) had called her from the beach. He couldn't breathe and might be having a heart attack.

I thought to myself... boy is she being a little dramatic... She could have waited a few more minutes for me to check out... This couldn't be so serious that it would warrant a return trip across island to retrieve the needed groceries that we had so abruptly left with the clerk.

As these thoughts flew through my consciousness in short fragments, Dorit talked about what Joe had said and she was clearly worried. Joe had called Dorit, told her (in short, labored gasps) that he couldn't breathe, his pulse was racing and that he might be having a heart attack.

I reassessed my position and decided that this was serious. There was definitely reason for concern.

Our car trip from Bailey's across the island to their home seemed to take forever. It was April and although visitors were beginning to return north, it was still a bumper-to-bumper car ride on a two lane road slowly moving toward Joe who was in trouble.

I began thinking, we should have called an ambulance. Certainly they could have made more progress in less time than we were. I started to really worry. I felt really anxious. What if he was dying?

Joe is my "little brother". He is a tall, strong man who works out regularly. While I don't think he's in perfect health, he seems in good shape for sixty-three. Of course, like the rest of us (myself and our other two sisters) he is always trying to lose those extra couple of pounds.

He was on the beach walking on that particular morning, training for a planned trek to Nepal. He is adventurous and had been around the world on many challenging "vacations". He and Dorit and their oldest child, Jacob, had recently completed a climb of Mt. Kilimanjaro.

Dorit and I talked continually, weighing the odds that this was something catastrophic. Because I wasn't willing to consider that, I reassured her that this was probably nothing really serious and we would find Joe in fine shape.

I felt confident because Joe can be a health "worrier". He was probably just exaggerating. I talked myself into a nice serene calm. Dorit wasn't buying it entirely.

Finally we got there. Joe was standing at the end of the beach access road, very near their home. He was indeed out of breath and he looked scared. His eyes were wide and pleading. He was sweating. He was holding his arm and taking his pulse.

Wow, I had not expected this. I was suddenly scared. We tried to get him in the car for the short drive to the house. He refused. Dorit asked about going to the hospital. Should she drive? Should she call an ambulance? Joe was not going.

He reported that he was breathing easier (than at onset) and that his pulse had slowed. He felt sure that the crisis had passed and that he would be fine. I was not so sure. If he was fine, how labored had his breath been fifteen minutes before? I really felt that he should be checked.

We got home and somehow Joe got up the flight of stairs to the main level of the house. This was Friday afternoon. Joe's breathing was still labored and any exertion at all caused real deep draws for breath. It was scary to sit by and watch but even more so, to listen.

Joe seemed scared. He checked his pulse regularly. He discussed his symptoms. Yet he flatly refused to "bother" any medical personnel until regular hours on Monday. He had called his doctor and had made an appointment on Monday. There was a long weekend ahead of us.

Joe was very quiet. He seemed absorbed in his survival. He was better (not breathing as heavily) when he was seated and inactive. As the weekend days passed by, Joe's symptoms didn't dissipate.

Dorit became immune and was almost dismissive of his complaints and comments. She mentioned to me that he "got worse" when he approached the stairs, intimating that he was adding drama to his situation. I understood her feelings, but I didn't agree with her. He couldn't breathe and this wasn't an act. However neither she nor Joe were doing anything until Monday and I had learned long ago not to argue with one stubborn person, let alone two.

It is an interesting phenomenon watching long married couples deal with medical problems. I had been married over thirty years and had been quickly willing to dismiss my husband's medical complaints and issues, until convinced otherwise.

Dorit's response seemed to me to be very normal. A long married, long suffering wife who had listened to a litany of complaints from children and spouse for years and was done with a compassionate response. Dorit wasn't cold hearted. She just didn't believe that Joe was quite as sick as he claimed to be.

I continued to be concerned. Joe was in trouble. I didn't like his breathing issues. I understand that I had significant breathing problems as an infant and somewhere deep in my memory, struggling to breathe resonates with my soul. I hated it. I was also present at the time of my mother's death, my father and I holding her as she struggled to breathe, gasping, eyes open and pleading, until the pulmonary embolism strangled her ability to breath and she lost the battle.

It is terrifying. I wanted Joe to get some help. I was anxious. I wanted him in some experienced medical hands, not with Dorit and me. That just wasn't going to happen. We were waiting "it" out!

Monday came. Dorit offered to go to the doctor with Joe. He declined the help/company. He went off alone. Dorit and I went on about our day. When we got home Joe was pleased to report that the doctor was taking a slow approach. The doctor had been made aware of Joe's leg problem (swelling, redness, hot bulge behind his knee) and the breathing crisis that had prompted the office visit. Nevertheless the doctor saw no need to rush. He scheduled an ultrasound for Wednesday.

REALLY? I was stunned. Joe was in crisis. He needed more help and he needed it now!

It wasn't going to happen. Another two days were in front of us and the waiting continued. Joe was stoic. He didn't complain but his breathing didn't improve. He was in distress. Though he accepted and actually seemed to appreciate his doctor's slow and cautious plan, I knew he was worried. Dorit stayed steady but somewhat removed. She had been reassured by the doctor's visit and was less concerned than she had been through the weekend.

I was glad to be with my family but there were constant silent questions which dominated all of our thoughts. What was happening to Joe? Was he going to be all right? Would he die?

Wednesday arrived, the day for the ultrasound and my return flight home. Once again, Joe declined Dorit's company for this medical test. Dorit was driving me to the airport when the phone rang. Joe said simply that the ultrasound had revealed a very large deep vein thrombosis behind his knee. He was being sent immediately to the hospital.

Though bad news, I was relieved that he was finally going to have the medical attention that he required!

Hearing how I presented my illness and reacted to it as seen through another's eyes I realize how self-defeating my behavior was. I had done nothing to help myself and instead played a game of pure chance with my life. But I also see we were all part of a process. Denial and diminishing the severity of the event and its aftermath was common to all of us.

CHAPTER TWO
HOSPITALIZATION

"The physician should not treat the disease but the patient who is suffering from it."

—*Maimonides*

(1135 -1204)

I had experienced a very large and life threatening pulmonary embolism that much was certain. I would find out subsequently that not only was the PE rare because of its size but also because it occurred without warning to an otherwise healthy individual. Most PEs, I learned later, strike individuals secondary to another serious medical condition. The majority too tend to be subacute, unrecognized at the time and often unknown until discovered long after the fact.

The number of people in the US who have a PE each year is a matter of considerable uncertainty, largely because the majority of instances are thought to be undiagnosed. In the months leading up to the major attack, as an example, I had an active DVT and labored breathing while exercising. So much so that my daughter once asked my wife why I was having so much trouble breathing after she and I had taken a walk together. It is not inconceivable that the DVTs were shedding small pieces for months prior to the main event, PEs that were never diagnosed or counted.

The best estimate from several sources of the incidence (new cases) of diagnosed PEs annually in the US is between 250,000 and 350,000 or approximately .7 to 1 case for every

1,000 residents. Added to this figure there may be as many as two to three times more undiagnosed cases per year or about another 650,000 incidents. Taken together then, perhaps as many as one million people living in the US have a PE each year. Most of these cases are secondary to a known risk factor such as immobility, surgery or cancer. Consequently, the majority of PEs occur in a hospital or long-term care setting.

Death rates among those who have a PE are quite high. In fact, pulmonary embolism ranks second only to heart attack as the leading cause of sudden death. The mortality rate of those stricken by a PE depends, not surprisingly, on the size of the clot. Nonmassive PEs (defined by the increase in arterial blood pressure going to the lungs) kill approximately 10% of the victims, whereas death among people with a massive PE, as mine was, occurs in the neighborhood of 50% of the time. Overall 30% will die as a result of an event. Death is most apt to occur in the first one to two hours after the attack, just the window of time when I walked home from the beach and decided to finish cleaning the garage.

Even in hospital settings where help is at hand, PEs kill with startling regularity. Some estimates suggest that 60% of all hospital deaths are attributable to PEs and 70% of these were not previously diagnosed. Pulmonary embolism has earned the sobriquet the "silent killer" as a consequence. The Centers for Disease Control and Prevention (CDC) provides a final, truly frightening statistic in this regard. In 25% of all cases of fatal pulmonary embolism, sudden death was the first symptom.

Once anticoagulation therapy begins, as happened when I was given a heparin injection in the ER after the PE diagnosis was confirmed, the risk of death declines rapidly to less than 5% of those treated. Nevertheless the all cause, one-year mortality for those who have had a PE is 24%, i.e., one in four people will expire in the year following the PE. Of course, many of these die from the same disease that caused the PE in the first place such as surgery complications, cancer or infection.

For those fortunate enough to survive, the body repairs itself swiftly. Within a week a third (36%) of clots in pulmonary arteries are resolved. The figure rises to half after two weeks and three-quarters by three months. Typically by six months the clots are resolved to the degree they ever will be, having dissolved completely and been reabsorbed by the body or become inert by calcifying and adhering to the vein. So the half-year milestone also marks the point when anticoagulation therapy ends in most cases.

Nonetheless while the threat is gone the impact lingers. Venous changes such as distended veins at the site of the clot particularly in the legs can create chronic difficulties raising the risk of subsequent DVT and PE episodes. So although I survived the first PE I would be at lifelong elevated risk for a recurrence, a circumstance that thankfully I was unaware of at the time. What I knew then was that I was in the hospital about to begin the long and arduous road to recovery however imperfect it might ultimately prove to be.

Before I could even settle into my new room on the Cardiac Ward though, I was besieged by a small army of caregivers who came through in the first hour. Nurses of every stripe, technicians, pharmacists, dietary staff, IV inserters, janitors, a primary care liaison and more came through to orient me to the rhythms of the ward and firmly fix me in its medical milieu. A blood pressure cuff encased my arm, a second IV was inserted, a blood oxygen meter clipped to my finger and a heart monitor suction cupped to my chest and belly. I was pinned like a butterfly in a display case.

It was a blinding whirlwind of single-focused people performing highly specialized tasks. There were so many roles and functions that a white board was hung within line of sight of the bed on which I lay, a Playbill providing the dramatis personae for the performance of the day and hour with the names of the actors and the parts they played scribbled on it. Being the leading man in the drama was a dubious honor to be sure.

Very early in my hospital stay I heard the notes to Twinkle, Twinkle Little Star broadcast over the hospital intercom. A nurse who was in the room at the time broke into a broad grin, drew my attention to the refrain and informed me that the notes were played every time a baby was born. In a ward where patients were tethered to life support machinery waiting for or recovering from extreme cardiac interventions, such as stents, bypasses, valve replacements and the like, it was an announcement from the opposite end of life, a joyous reaffirmation that life goes on and a bracing elixir to lift the spirits of a ward where people were gravely ill.

Undoubtedly the nurses, in addition to enjoying the moment themselves, knew the buoying effect the tune would have on the patients. Over time I assumed their role pointing out the significance to family and friends. That such a little thing could so easily transport one's thoughts beyond the mire of their own condition was one of the most powerful medicines administered in the hospital. It never ceased to be the bright spot in my day.

Hospitalists

Early in my assimilation into the cast, I was introduced to the director of the drama, the "Hospitalist." The Hospitalist in my case was a board certified Internist whose sole practice of medicine is confined within the walls of the hospital. The Hospitalist is the individual whose responsibility it was to manage my care during my stay, to develop a treatment plan, choose among therapeutic options, select and dose prescription drugs, marshal the requisite resources by arranging consultations with related specialists and so forth. The Hospitalist is the final authority when it comes to the patient's care and makes all the decisions about it.

Hospitalists wield a heavy hammer of authority. Once when I said I wanted to continue treatment at home even though my level of anticoagulation had not reached a therapeutic level, I was told the Hospitalist would release me when it was appropriate. Even the choice of verbs, "release", is revealing. I pointed out that I was a patient not a prisoner and could leave whenever I liked if I was ready to assume the risks and responsibilities of homecare. True enough agreed the nurses but under those circumstances the Hospitalist would record that I had left against medical advice. This, they warned, had the potential of allowing the insurance company to invalidate my hospital stay and to refuse to pay the associated costs.

With the hospital stay already costing in the tens of thousands of dollars, I was certain, and rising daily, this was a powerful incentive to toe the line and obey the Hospitalist.

The Hospitalist position and specialization is relatively new the name itself having entered the medical nomenclature as late as 1996. Conceptually it makes sense to have a single individual manage all the medical resources and treatment while a patient is in the hospital. It should be more efficient since it releases the patient's usual primary care physician from the time consuming task of making hospital rounds. The extramural physician can concentrate on office visits where they can treat patients before and after hospitalization, allowing a scarce resource, the physician's time, to be spread over a greater number in need.

As delivered however the Hospitalist concept leaves a great deal to be desired. In practice I found the Hospitalist to be largely a cadre of foreign medical graduates who were occupying the position as a stepping-stone to private practice, a foot in the door to the Great American Medical Bazaar. Untold riches lay beyond. They represented a polyglot of nationalities, a Tower of Babel mix of accents and fluency that did little to advance the doctor-patient communication and more often degraded it.

At the worst, Hospitalists became a sales force for the hospital, carrying a bag full of diagnostic tests, vaccinations and prescriptions to shill.

"Have you had a flu shot this year?"

"You have? Well a pneumonia vaccination is indicated for someone your age with compromised lung function."

"Whooping cough is on the increase. You probably need a booster."

"A full body CT scan will rule out cancer as the cause of your PE."

"Do you need any painkillers? How about something to help you sleep?

"Your CT scan shows a dark area on the tail of your pancreas. It needs to be examined immediately. I will schedule an MRI."

The preceding were just some of the approaches that were made to me for added services, tests and drugs. All were rebuffed in favor of post-hospital consultations with the physicians with whom I had a pre-emergency relationship. But as a former marketing expert I admired the perseverance of the Hospitalists. It is always most profitable to sell more to existing customers especially those in mid transaction. "Want fries with that?" My treatment was being super-sized.

The skills of the Hospitalists varied greatly by country of origin. Indians were the best trained, easiest to communicate with and most attentive to the patient in my experience. They were willing to sit for long periods, more than the perfunctory two minute look-ins of other Hospitalists anyway, to take a history or listen to how the disease and recovery were perceived by the patient. Indian physicians, I felt, were much less apt to dismiss my complaints and observations with vacuous reassurances.

Physicians from Central America, the Caribbean or South America were all energy it seemed. They blew into my room unexpectedly, strew medical opinions about, leaving a debris field of orders and instructions and blew out again. They were the Hospitalist equivalent of subtropical weather disturbances, gales or hurricanes.

Hospitalists from Eastern Europe and the former Soviet Union were well trained, in my opinion, but a certain authoritarianism followed in their wake. The patient was a necessary evil that legitimated their position. They were the least likely to share or discuss medical findings as a result.

In one instance, the aptly named Dr. Badov was assigned to me. I requested a copy of the CT scan of my chest from him so I could read it. He at first ignored the request and tried to comfort me by saying that I would be fine. When I persisted he put his hand on my shoulder softly and inquired whether I felt I was really capable of understanding the report. I assured him I was and more forcefully pressed the claim to my medical records, at which point Dr. Badov wheeled around and left the room, never to return again. Five minutes later a nurse delivered the report.

Two Hospitalists who attended me were native born and educated in the U.S. One came in immediately after admission to explain to me how the Hospitalist system worked. It was a five minute consultation. I never saw her again. Coming and going was the norm for Hospitalists. The second took over my care after the aforementioned Dr. Badov chose to absent himself. U.S. trained physicians seemed to be much less threatened by a patient who demanded records, a discussion of options or who wanted answers to questions about their status and prognosis. These physicians were also easier for me to communicate with since we shared a set of cultural touchstones and references. The expectations and communication between doctor and patient was improved commensurately.

In the end the issue with the foreign medical graduates was less a matter of medical competence than the pervasiveness of culture. The foreign trained physicians were a product of their backgrounds and what that implied about how they expected to conduct the doctor-patient relationship.

But as powerful as culture proved to be in adding a patina, glossy or matte, to physician patient interactions, there is something more pernicious built into the nature of the Hospitalist position, I believe, that creates an impediment to care independent of the training and skills of the practitioner. The Hospitalist is assigned to the patient without their input or consent. By design they are interjected between the patient and his usual providers with whom he may have a long-term relationship, causing a disruption in the normal routine of patient care. It is as if the patient is new born into the medical system and must learn their way again.

The Hospitalist is moreover a physician not of the patient's choosing. No vetting has gone on, and there is no way to check their abilities. Hospitalists have no knowledge or understanding of a patient's history that can be taken for granted and used as a foundation for treatment. Most important of all, there is no reservoir of trust to draw on. When a patient most needs familiarity, confidence and trust they are forced to deal with a physician they know nothing about, whose expertise is in question and who they may not have agreed to if given the choice.

What complicates the situation further is that patient may be asked to make major life decisions regarding treatment options. Options the consequences of which they may not fully understand. Ones that present differential risks and benefits that need to be weighed in the context of the patient's life circumstances since lifestyle adjustments are called for more often than not.

The patient, even when included in these decisions, which is not a given by any means, is at an informational disadvantage. Usually they have little if any understanding of their disease, the mechanics by which it operates and threatens them. Having spent the majority of my professional career working in medical settings or researching medical topics, I considered myself to be a knowledgeable patient. Despite all my experience something as basic as the fact that I was placed in a Cardiac Ward even though I had a pulmonary (lung) embolism was puzzling to me. Only after a quick trip to the Internet did I learn the forehead slap obvious, a pulmonary embolism affects blood flow to and from the lungs not the flow of air in and out of them.

If patients have imperfect knowledge of their disease, they are probably even less well informed about the treatment options that are available. They may not even know alternatives exist to the one prescribed by the Hospitalist. In my experience there was no discussion of alternatives, the efficacy, side effects and risks associated with each and the kind of lifestyle accommodations that were required, a major consideration in the case of anticoagulation therapy. Unless informed and counseled by the physician, patients cannot hope to evaluate the alternatives accurately in the context of their own lives, and to determine what makes the most sense for them.

The Internet has leveled the informational playing field to some degree. But access to information does not necessarily translate into acquisition and comprehension of it. Moreover what information can be gleaned from the Internet is offset by the explosive growth of the medical literature. With such rapid advances in medical research, pharmacology and treatment protocols, I suspect even physicians have difficulty keeping current.

I was fortunate in many regards. My daughter Jane, who by the oddest coincidence had come to town for a visit and was just landing as I was driving myself to the ER, watched the cacophony of care that swirled around me and saw my increasingly frustrating interaction with the Hospitalist. She realized I was not getting answers to basic questions about my health status and prognosis. How bad was it? Was I still in danger? How long would I have to be in the hospital? How long would the recovery be? Most importantly, would I recover fully?

Seeing where the situation was headed – frustration and recrimination – Jane took matters in hand. She called a friend who in turn put Jane in touch with her father, a prominent and well-respected, local Radiologist. A brief conversation followed, filled with admonitions, instructions and promises of help. As promised, within a half hour the lead Pulmonologist in the hospital showed up on my doorstep and the attitude toward me, the patient, changed substantially and for the better.

The Pulmonologist was clearly an individual who commanded great respect among other practitioners including the Hospitalist who deferred to his judgment. For the length of my stay I basked in the aura of respect that surrounded him and to my benefit rubbed off on me. There was an unspoken change in the demeanor of those caring for me. I was now a patient to notice, to accommodate if at all possible. After all I had demonstrated clout. I could summon the best resources available outside the usual procurement channels and without consulting the Hospitalist. I could only imagine what a person without contacts would experience and I was grateful.

A room full of physicians, nurses and technicians seemed to melt away as the Pulmonologist began his consultation. He listened attentively and without interruption as I gave a history of the emergency. He then dispassionately gave me an assessment of my current situation. It was not punctuated with any excess emotions or comments such as "You are lucky to be alive." For the first time I learned that the embolism was massive; that had it been a centimeter larger it would have caused my heart to stop beating and that 10-20% of my lung had died and would not recover.

What mattered the most to me at the time was my prognosis, how long would it take to recover and what restrictions would there be on my lifestyle? Even at this late date and with all I knew and had just been told, I still had expectations of making the trip to Mt. Kailash for the May festival, just five weeks away. When I told the doctor the trip figured significantly in my decision calculus, I was met with a look of stunned amazement and a chuckle of disbelief. I was quickly disabused of the notion of any travel in the foreseeable future. He pointed out to me that there was no obvious cause for the DVT that shed the embolism. Because it was idiopathic or "unprovoked" as he put it, I would need to be on anticoagulants for at least six months if not a year and the associated risks of travel to a place where the air was thin, medical attention was days away and the chances of falling were quite high was not advisable during that time.

Then in an avuncular manner the Pulmonologist dropped more bad news. Given the permanent damage to my lung it was unlikely that I would ever be able to climb to high altitudes again. Scuba diving and the changes in pressure that compress the lungs at increasing depth was definitely out. Sympathetic to my obvious disappointment he tried to bargain with me. I could, he said, go to the bottom of the Grand Canyon and hike out if I needed a strenuous climb, but an uphill hike in thin air was out of the question.

This was the first inkling I was given of how my life would change – substantially – how it would be more circumscribed and limited in the future. Many more were to follow. The biggest of these was derived from the implications of the therapeutic regimen I would be put on in order to heal. It would require that I accommodate to the peculiarities of the medicine with a series of significant lifestyle changes, ones that would dramatically alter my previous nonchalant and carefree approach to health. Now adjusting to the medicine would become the preoccupation, driving, often monopolizing my life, becoming a fear-forced obsession.

The choice of the appropriate anticoagulant also became the flashpoint for all the simmering dissatisfactions I felt about the Hospitalists. It was the perfect cyclone of misunderstanding where the needs and fears of a frightened, anxious, and ill-informed patient came into bitter conflict with the established therapeutic protocol taken for granted by the Hospitalists and with their customary modes of patient care. It was played out in an arena where the antagonists did not communicate well and there was no foundation familiarity and trust. In the end it was a question of who would make the healthcare decisions.

Coumadin

Much of my stay in the hospital involved coming to terms both physically and psychologically with anticoagulation therapy and the drug of choice, Warfarin or as it is known by its trade name Coumadin. In fact, the hospital stay could be viewed as an enforced waiting period while the drug built up in my system to a therapeutic level. At which point I could be released with little fear of relapse. If I stayed compliant, taking the drug as prescribed, only limited ongoing professional care and supervision would be needed to determine periodically if the drug was at therapeutic levels.

The journey of Warfarin from identification to wonder drug is a fascinating story in its own right. Warfarin was discovered the old fashion way, by observing a problem in the natural world and isolating the causal factor in a lab. The interesting twist in the Warfarin story is the presence of a great insight that allowed a scientist to recognize that a deadly chemical could be used to save lives. Along the way a great deal of serendipity entered in, not unlike with the discovery of penicillin. Warfarin and penicillin, two drugs that have saved countless millions of lives in the last half of the 20th Century, are related coincidentally on a more fundamental level. Both are by-products of the digestive action of fungi.

Early in the 1920's farms in the upper Midwest were plagued by an unknown ailment that caused livestock to bleed to death spontaneously, after injury or when subjected to normal animal husbandry practices such as dehorning or castration. Not all farms were affected and animals on unaffected farms remained universally healthy. This difference in distribution of the disease created an opportunity to identify the source of the problem. As early as 1921 Canadian veterinarian Paul Schofield established that diseased and dying animals were fed "spoiled" sweet clover, i.e., plants with broken stems that provided a food source for fungus to feed on and grow, whereas healthy animals were fed unspoiled clover.

That's where the matter stood for a decade, with a known source by no known cause. It stayed that way until 1935 when a dairy farmer arrived at the University of Wisconsin and dropped off cans containing bloody milk and a pile of silage made up of spoiled sweet clover. A university scientist, Karl Paul Link, recognized an opportunity in the unusual donations and spent the next five years working with his assistant Harold Campbell to isolate the chemical that caused the animals to bleed spontaneously. The anticoagulation chemical isolated was coumarin, which was given to the Wisconsin Alumni Research Foundation (WARF) for commercial exploitation. The chemical was renamed Warfarin, to establish a connection to coum-arin.

But Link was not done. He recognized that a chemical that killed cattle would surely kill smaller animals in smaller doses. As Link said, "From the beginning I had an intuitive feeling that this might be a good thing. A pretty bad thing for rats, but a good thing for humans." Warfarin was approved for use as a rodenticide in 1948.

Then another strange event occurred that propelled Warfarin on the path to being one of the most widely used and beneficial drugs of all time. In 1951 a soldier in the U.S. Army tried to commit suicide by ingesting Warfarin. His life was saved however by an administration of Vitamin K proving that the effects of Warfarin could be controlled and reversed if need be, thereby making it safe for human use. The FDA approved Warfarin for human use in 1954 and it was marketed under the trade name Coumadin[2]. Interestingly, one of the first patients to use Coumadin was President Eisenhower who was given the drug following a heart attack in 1955.

Since its certification for human use a great deal has been learned about how Coumadin produces its anticoagulation effect. Vitamin K is a primary agent in the clotting process since it affects a number of steps in the cascade of hemalogical changes that cause a clot to form in the presence of injury or slow moving blood. Coumadin operates by interrupting this process, specifically by slowing the metabolism and reabsorption of Vitamin K, delaying the body's ability to recycle its store of Vitamin K after the initial use. Less Vitamin K is available for reuse thereby slowing the ability of blood to clot. The effect does not thin blood per se and Coumadin is not a blood thinner, as it is colloquially understood since the viscosity of the blood stays the same. Rather and more precisely the effect is one of anticoagulation.

Being a Vitamin K antagonist differentiates Coumadin from other types of anticoagulants. Drugs like aspirin, ibuprofen (Advil, Aleve) or Plavix, so called nonsteroidal anti-inflammation drugs (NSAIDs) prevent clots by inhibiting platelets from adhering to each other and in so doing forming a clot. NSAIDs are more effective therefore in preventing clotting

---

[2] Hereafter I use Coumadin to refer equally to warfarin since they are pharmaceutically identical.

of fast moving arterial blood and hence are used prophylactically and therapeutically to prevent and treat artery-related cardiac problems, chief among those being heart attack, stroke, and peripheral artery disease. Coumadin, by contrast, inhibits the clotting properties of Vitamin K, which requires pooled or slow moving blood to form a clot. As such Coumadin is more apt to be used to treat venous related diseases, such DVTs, PEs and diseases that cause poor blood flow such as atrial fibrillation.

In practice anticoagulation is measured by how slowly a person's blood coagulates when compared to a common standard. Prothrombin time (PT) measures an individual's clotting time and this in turn is compared to the standard and converted into a ratio. The resulting International Standardized Ratio (INR) indicates the degree of anticoagulation a person has. Too low and the patient does not have a therapeutic level of Coumadin in their system indicating they are at risk to form additional blood clots. Conversely, an INR too high suggests the patient is at risk for unprovoked bleeding incidents some of which can be life threatening as I was to find out.

An INR of 1.0 indicates that the patient has the same clotting time as the standard, in other words, the clotting time of a normal person. An INR of 2.0 means it takes twice as long for the patient to form a clot when compared with the standard, and INR of 3.0 three times as long and so forth. The typical therapeutic INR range for a person suffering with DVTs or PEs is from 2.0 to 3.0. In that narrow range the patient is relatively safe, protected against clot formation and excessive bleeding; allowing the body time to create alternative circulatory pathways around the clot, a process known as canalization, or for the clot to dissolve and be reabsorbed, a process that begins rapidly but can take a full six months to complete.

Staying within the range is tricky however. Coumadin is a notoriously finicky drug and INR levels can vary not only by dosage but also for any number of other reasons such as diet or drug interactions. Frequent blood tests are needed to confirm a person's INR is within the therapeutic range and tinkering with dosage is required if it is not. The drug regimen is inconvenient at best of times.

Long-term Coumadin use is no walk in the park either. In particular, a diet high in Vitamin K rich foods can reduce the anticoagulation properties of Coumadin. That is, the higher the amount of Vitamin K circulating in the blood, the greater the dose of Coumadin needed to raise the INR above the therapeutic threshold and keep it there. As a consequence there are myriad dietary restrictions. Many foods inhibit the effects of the drug since they contain large quantities of Vitamin K. Green leafy vegetables; spinach, kale, lettuce, cabbage, etc. are the worst offenders. Other green vegetables, peas, cucumbers, green beans, Brussel Sprouts are lesser villains. In fact, if it's green odds are it's verboten.

Now limiting consumption of these foods may seem like being thrown in the briar patch by some folks, but for those of us who subsist mostly by eating foliage, it can be difficult to navigate around favorite foods. It is too, I might add, stultifying boring to look at a plate of beige every meal. After a while it is enough to bring suicidal ideation about ending it all by binging on an enormous spinach salad swimming in Green Goddess dressing.

Then, of course, there are foods that have exactly the opposite effect. Alcohol as an example potentiates the effect of Coumadin. Many other drugs are out because they either increase bleeding risks, e.g. aspirin or interact with Coumadin, e.g. antibiotics. And of course it goes almost without saying grapefruit is a no-no. But then grapefruit interacts badly with just about any drug. It is the universal pharmacological bad actor apparently.

All these problems are well known. Medical professionals are also quick to point out the banned foods because they effect the efficacy of the drug and hence the therapeutic value. Virtually every doctor who has discussed Coumadin use with me has admonished me to simply do the same thing every day because the therapeutic dose of Coumadin can be adjusted to take into account the effect of the foods eaten. Want a glass of wine with dinner – no problem. Just make sure you have the same amount every day. Want to gorge on green beans – no problem either, just eat the same amount every day. This, of course, is humanly impossible, which is one reason why INR testing on a regular basis is required.

What medical professionals do not readily divulge I found is the host of nasty side effects that accompany Coumadin use. Muscle aches, fever and flu-like symptoms, weight gain, rashes, itching, stiffness and difficulty moving are some of the side effects I experienced and still do. Two of my least favorites are hair loss, in my case a natural process I do not care to accelerate, and anxiety. With respect to the later I maintain that I can give a close approximation to my INR level just by how anxious I am when falling asleep or by the anxiety-ridden dreams that follow. There is such a wide range of side effects that whenever I feel out of sorts I rush to Wikipedia, WebMD or the like and more often than not Coumadin is the culprit.

The side effect that strikes fear in the hearts of all users of Coumadin and their physicians is uncontrolled bleeding. It is a well-earned reputation. Coumadin-related bleeding account for 29,000 emergency room visits annually in the U.S., fully 4% of the 700,000 Adverse Drug Events (ADEs). This figure rises to 16% of ADEs for those over the age of 50 and 33% for people 65 years old or older. The overall mortality rate from Coumadin-related bleeding is estimated to be 1-3% of users each year. Uncontrolled, even fatal bleeding is always the ghost in the closet Coumadin users fear. But of all the people I knew who were taking the drug no one ever had a bleeding episode of this severity—that is, until I had one.

Despite all the drawbacks, Coumadin has a number of benefits that outweigh them. The drug is ridiculously inexpensive by contemporary pharmacological standards, less than a dollar a day in most cases. A real bargain especially when the downside is the possibility of more DVTs or another potentially life-ending PE. Another advantage is: since Coumadin takes time to build up to a therapeutic level, it conversely takes time to decrease to a nontherapeutic one if stopped, a major benefit for those of us who are prone to forget a daily dose. Residual Coumadin levels continue to protect us while we come to our senses.

And the greatest benefit of all – Coumadin effects are reversible if need be. This property distinguishes Coumadin from a number of new anticoagulant medicines that are coming on the market, e.g., Pradaxa and Xarelto, the anticoagulation effect of which can only be negated when out of control by a full cleaning of the blood by dialysis. An out-of-control Coumadin bleeding event, however, can be stopped with the administration of Vitamin K and a transfusion of blood clotting factors found in plasma. The reversibility property can be a life saver. I know because, like an anonymous soldier 60 years ago, it saved mine.

So Coumadin has been the standard of care for hypercoagulative disorders for the past 60 years. Estimates of current usage are vague but there may be as many as 20 million active Coumadin users in the U.S. alone accounting for 20-30 million prescriptions for the drug per year. Another 2 million new users are added to the rolls annually according to the FDA. Coumadin use increases with age so it is nearly impossible for a person my age not to know someone, more likely many people, who are on the drug "for life" or who have taken the medicine for a period of time.

Before hospitalization what I knew about Coumadin came from conversations with these people. It was very impressionistic and spotty. Bleeding and easy bruising were often mentioned annoyances as were inconveniences associated with the drug's use, avoidance of activities that might result in falling and precipitate a significant bleed especially in the cranium being the most often mentioned. But the benefits were clear too – the biggest of which was the lore-giver was still alive. Now it was my turn to learn firsthand.

My in-going impressions were also complicated by my attitudes, most of them subtly pejorative, toward the people who took anticoagulants and specifically Coumadin. My preconception was: Coumadin users are sick, physically vulnerable, and weak – worst of all they are old. They suffered from a chronic disease, one that required taking medicine daily, and would require that they spending their remaining lives tethered to a chemical life-line. In short, in my view, Coumadin use was symbolic of decline, the passing from the prime of life to the frailty of old age. It signaled moving from being vital, relevant, a person of account, someone who mattered to an invisible person slumping to irrelevance and death.

That certainly was not the way I saw myself. As I evaluated my situation, I was not someone with a chronic disease. I was the unfortunate victim of a serious vascular accident that would take time to heal. But heal it would and heal completely. I had many serious athletic injuries in my life. This was no different. When it was over I would be just as capable, adventuresome and significant as before – a force to be reckoned with – at least in my mind's eye. I was not ready to give in to decline and when I did I would rage against the dying of the light. Anticoagulants were a necessary bridge to get me from damaged to whole. A crutch I would discard as soon as practicable as if it were a cast on a broken limb.

To alter my lifestyle was tantamount to surrendering to the tyranny of the drug. I had no intention of doing so. I would not accommodate to the vagaries of the drug. I would take a drug that required no accommodation at all. In fact, I was already on one, Lovenox, a low molecular weight heparin product. Looking at the strictures imposed by Coumadin, Lovenox was carefree alternative. There are no dietary restrictions, no INR testing, fewer side effects, lower bleeding risk, and even an antidote should there ever be a serious bleeding event. If that were not enough to decide the matter, anticoagulation is immediate, no hospital stay required while the drug builds up to a therapeutic level.

What's not to like? Well a few things actually. Lovenox requires twice daily injections in the subcutaneous fat surrounding the lower abdomen. Because the drug stops clotting instantly on contact, bleeding at the injection site is commonplace. One week of use in the hospital and my spare tire was transformed into an obi of vivid royal purple bruises.

Then there is the cost – $100 per shot. Two injections per day added up to $73,000 per year for the privilege of staying healthy by my calculation. Coumadin – at a dollar a day, is a mere $365 per year. Even factoring in $50 INR tests twice a month and the annual cost of therapy between Coumadin and Lovenox still is no contest. I had an inkling my insurance carrier might balk at the differential. In the first few days of my hospital stay however three months was the length of time I was told I would probably be on anticoagulants. $18,000 – that might be doable.

Given the cost benefit calculus, it might be fair to ask why I resisted Coumadin so ferociously. Naturally there was my on-going delusion that what I experienced was a temporary setback, a speed bump along the road I wanted to travel. Maybe I would not make the Saga Dawa festival that May, but certainly I would the following year. I expected, demanded even, a complete cure and return to my former activities. It was impossible for me to accept a reality in which I might be permanently damaged.

But more than that, this was a decision that affected my life. It was my right to make it. My health after all was on the line and therefore my decision was final. I intended to make an affirmative choice not just accept one that had been made for me. This intransigence brought me into direct conflict with established treatment protocols, the dependable rhythms of hospital operations and ultimately into vehement disagreement with the authority of the Hospitalists.

It all started in the first twelve hours after admission when one of the nurses came into my room and handed me a Dixie cup containing two pills. I asked what they were. Coumadin I was told as if the name alone would provide the rationale for taking them. I refused the medicine, pointing out in the process that no one had as yet discussed a treatment regimen with me. Until I understood what the plan was and I agreed with it I would not take any new medicines. The nurse was nonplussed and left to find the Hospitalist.

Next up was the Hospitalist. She came into the room and asked what the matter was. I explained I knew little about

Coumadin and what I did know was not comforting. My opinion was Lovenox provided a comparable, in some ways superior, level of anticoagulation without requiring any of the inevitable behavior modification associated with Coumadin use. I preferred to use Lovenox going forward. A good case and better summation, if you ask me.

She continued to insist Coumadin was the standard of care. The argument was not really about choice of medicine, it was about who had the authority to determine what drug would be used. The more she refused to recognize the validity of my wishes, the more it became clear I would have no say in the decision and the angrier I got.

Finally, I said, "I have never met you before today. I know nothing about you. With any luck I will leave here in a few days and we will never need to see each other again." I continued, "My primary care physician will be responsible for my treatment from then on. So he and I will make the decision about the medicine that is best for me." Pretty harsh I know. But I was pretty pissed.

To her credit the Hospitalist took the tirade in stride and continued to press her case. She eventually hit on a point that resonated. One that allowed me to feel, at least for a day, that I was in charge and I was making the decision. Coumadin took time to accumulate and reach a therapeutic level, she pointed out, and a characteristic of the drug I knew and accepted. If I took that day's dose I could begin treatment while the decision was made. I would not have to extend the hospital stay if Coumadin was the ultimate decision. I took the Dixie cup and swallowed the pills. With a truce in effect the Hospitalist left to continue her rounds.

I took the opportunity to place a call to my primary care physician so we could discuss the matter. After leaving a message I settled in to wait for a call back. It came a number of hours later at the end of the work day. He launched into the conversation by informing me that he had spoken to the Hospitalist and they both agreed Coumadin was the appropriate therapeutic agent.

I was appalled. I felt betrayed. My long-standing relationship with my primary care physician, the touchstone of my interaction with the medical community had been usurped. The Hospitalist had, without my permission, intruded into what I considered to be a private doctor-patient relationship. She had in the process cut me out of the decision.

The doctor listened patiently while I shared my perspective with him. My chief objective was to change my life as little as possible so I could resume my old ways seamlessly when the clots were resolved. I expressed my opinion that Lovenox was the drug least likely to disrupt my life. This prompted an impassioned soliloquy by my doctor on the pros and cons of the two options, including several downsides of Lovenox use I had not known such as the possibility of liver problems with long term use. He addressed my concerns about leading a circumscribed life and assured me it was not as onerous as I imagined. His case was compelling I had to admit. But then I was also more apt to accept it from him. So we were agreed—Coumadin it was. I was satisfied in the end. If I had not made the decision I had at least been part of the decision-making.

The next day, the hapless Hospitalist, unaware of my calls, came to my room to inform me that she had spoken to my primary care physician and he agreed with her judgment that Coumadin was the preferred treatment. Rather than reassure me as she no doubt expected it would, it pushed all my buttons. I was livid. She continued to fail to see the validity of my claim to be part of the decision. She viewed the situation as a patient management matter, which it was. But for her it was a question of medical authority and hence her solution to the impasse had been to call my physician to enlist his aid in convincing me. For my part the issue was also a question of authority, but in my universe the patient ruled—my body, my call.

I lit into her, quite savagely I'm ashamed to say. "I know you spoke to my doctor," I started, speaking through clenched teeth. "I want you to know I consider this to be an egregious violation of the doctor-patient relationship, since I told you I would make the decision with my Internist," I continued. Then

I summarily fired her. "I want you off my case. Send in the head Hospitalist".

Looking back I realize this was not malicious on her part, Coumadin was the gold standard. It was efficacious, dosing protocols were worked out for nearly every manifestation of my disease, and for every type of patient. I was bucking a proven remedy. She had, I am sure, never met anyone before who questioned their doctor, let alone one of the most reliable protocols in modern medicine and she was unprepared no doubt to deal with the push back. I wish I could have been more appreciative of her perspective, a failing I was more than ready to point out when our positions were reversed.

Throughout the episode I was, I will readily admit, very hard to deal with, something of an arrogant prick to be candid. While I was able to intellectualize the debate over treatment options in order to give a reasoned basis for my recalcitrance, to transform and morph it in a sense into a moral stand in defense of high principles, in fact a good part of my motivation was naked, gut emptying fear. I could not let myself deal with the reality that lurked in the recesses of my mind. I was petrified of having a second PE, of once again balancing breathless on the cusp between life and death.

Occasionally my defenses would crack a bit and the terror would glare through. The memory of what it was like to be the fish on the line was so debilitating I had to force it back into its subconscious cage with every psychological trick I could conjure. During the attack I had no time to consider the consequences of what was happening. Now I did but I was not ready. It was too close, too fresh. So I shielded myself behind a cloak of high purpose walking a schizophrenic line between denial and dread, the thin path between arrogance and angst.

In the final analysis all the remonstrations about which medicine to take reduced to a matter of control. I desperately needed to believe I could affect my circumstances, to move them in the direction I pointed. I wanted to believe if only I took personal charge of my recovery, I could guarantee a positive outcome. I could effect a complete recovery, prevent any future occurrences and ultimately keep myself from dying.

Moreover I was in the best position to make it happen because I had the most at stake. Everybody else, with the possible exception of my immediate family there beside me, the doctors, nurses, technicians had competing demands on their attention, but not me. I was ever vigilant always on guard for any sign a repeat accident was imminent. No one else was that invested in my well-being. Others were much more apt to miss something important, to let something slip through the safety net to disastrous end. I was convinced.

At this point I was already starting to wonder why this had happened to me. I was beginning to construct the mental scaffolding of victimization causality—the belief that I would not be in this predicament had my primary care physician been more attentive to my pre-attack symptoms. Had he ordered a simple diagnostic test in time the entire life-threatening event could have been avoided. If only the conditions leading up to the attack had been recognized and acted upon I would not be where I found myself at that moment. I was determined not to let his happen again.

This kind of magical thinking can have the opposite effect though when sound and learned advice is ignored. There is an old adage in advertising, a self-justifying one, to the effect that clients get the agency they deserve. In many respects I felt the same way about patients—they get the medical care they demand. Maybe I should have paid more heed to a less self-serving aphorism from another profession—a lawyer who represents himself has a fool for a client. But this would be resolved in due time.

The remainder of the hospitalization passed uneventfully. Ultimately the head Hospitalist took my case personally. Our relationship was much more that of equals, collegial, respectful and pleasant until my discharge. While hospitalized I had been tested for nearly every possible related ailment and potential risk factor for PE's, chemical, genetic and physical. They all came up negative leaving the reason for the PE unexplained. My INR rose to therapeutic levels. I was free to go.

Auspiciously, the morning of my discharge Twinkle, Twinkle, Little Star played thirteen times, on one occasion back-to-back – twins.

CHAPTER THREE
THE NEW NORMAL—
PTSD AND TREATMENT

"I should point out – PTSD results when a person has
their deluded belief they're going to live forever
stripped away from them."

—Alex Lickerman, M.D.

(1966 -)

Night was always the most fearsome time. I quickly learned to dread twilight, usually a time of peace, glorious muted colors and shimmering accents on the water. It became instead a time of growing fear and rising anxiety. The darkness of night was beginning to envelope me. Sight, the most immediate window to the world and information laden sense, was about to be diminished, limited to shadows. The other senses would take over, filling the information deficit, but this only made me more conscious of the tactile inputs from throughout my body. The twinges, stabs of pain, dull aches that appeared and went for no reason I could discern.

Night was more than that. It was death's rehearsal, presaging the time when everything would go dark forever. Night was the time when I lived in my mind and the demons that resided there were difficult to keep at bay. Lying in the dark, wondering about the night to come, would it be easy—sleeping through till dawn or would I wake at 1, 2, or 3AM, look at the clock and realize that I had hours to go until it was over.

Wondering, why did I wake? Was anything wrong? Would I live until morning?

Turning on the light never seemed to help much. At some point I would have to turn it off again and reset the mental waiting clock that measured the time that would need to pass until daylight. Lamplight was never an adequate substitute for sunlight. In the night I often wondered what would happen if I had another PE. When daylight came it was easy to repress this thought, start the day with the expectation that I would be all right until the next evening. Seeing the light slowly, slowly grow in my room was accompanied by growing hope, and relief that soon I would be released from the ordeal that night had become.

Dreams were the demons of the night. For some reason I seemed to remember them more readily after the accident than before. The memory of them was often incomplete, just fleeting snippets, flashes of the characters that inhabited them, or residues of the emotions they conjured. Many were terribly violent with me exacting revenge on someone or something. Just as often the reverse was true. Some were specific to my disease, vivid dreams of finding the veins in my legs articulated by rock hard clots that ran its full length. Few dreams were pleasant or ones I wished I could return to.

Death dreams were the category I learned to dread the most but surprisingly there was also an element of mystery to them. There were ones that precipitated nothing less than night terrors. I would wake in a start with vague recollections of having dreamed about my own mortality. But this was drowned out by the tactile senses. My skin crawled, jumping as if electrically stimulated. My blood ran cold. Hackneyed expression both I know but I can find no better description of what I felt. I worried that my autonomic reaction was so strong it would overwhelm my weakened heart causing the death I subconsciously feared. And with these sensory storms came the anxiety, the profound sense of foreboding, not necessarily of the present or the immediate future, but of the realization that an indefinable condition lay at the end of life—nonexistence—and I was getting ever closer to it.

At times death dreams were symbolic and loaded with allegorical significance. One I recalled quite completely. When I awoke it was transparent and easy to interpret. I was walking on a vast rolling landscape of treeless, verdant hills, a trek that was not arduous but long. I came to the shore of a lake and stood on the sand and pebble strewn shore looking out across the flat surface that extended as far as I could see in all directions. The land just came to an end; I had reached a point where I could go no farther. The water in turn extended into the distance until vanishing in the limitless horizon. There was no place left for me to go other than to enter the water, but I hesitated. What would swimming in the lake be like? Would it be cold and inhospitable or comfortably warm? What lay beneath the opaque surface? It doesn't take a mystic, prophet or a psychiatrist to identify the symbolic referent of this dream.

PTSD

Sleep disorders were just one of many physical, mental and social sequelae that emerged in the months following the pulmonary embolism, examples of a constellation of symptoms and complaints that have been collected under the label Post-traumatic stress disorder (PTSD). Originally associated with the diffuse malaise and mental problems seen among combat veterans, PTSD has become something of a cause célèbre in recent years as it became clear that other groups of individuals are likely to present the same manifestations after experiencing or witnessing a traumatic life threatening event.

The American Psychiatric Association (APA), the arbiter of such things, defines PTSD as: exposure to actual or threatened death, serious injury or sexual violation. Exposure in turn can come as a function of:

- Direct experience
- Witnessing an event
- Learning about one affecting a family member or close friend, or

- Repeated firsthand exposure to the details of such an event.

Given the broad and inclusive nature of the definition a large swath of the population could be candidates for PTSD at any particular time. To name a few of the at-risk groups: combat veterans, first responders, heart attack survivors, rape victims, jury members in trials involving graphic descriptions of violent crimes, torture victims, and not to be exclude myself, survivors of massive pulmonary embolisms, as well as the family and friends of these individuals. It must be a sheltered life indeed that does not involve an exposure to a PTSD generating event at some time or another.

Prevalence

PTSD is not a widespread disorder but in terms of the number of people affected it represents a significant public health problem. The prevalence of PTSD has been measured twice as part of the National Comorbidity Study, a nationally representative survey of mental disease among adults in the US, initially fielded in 1990-1992 and again in 2001-2003. The most recent survey estimated that 3.6% of American adults 18 years or older either had PTSD at the time of the survey or did have it in the preceding year, with women being nearly three times more likely than men to have PTSD, 5.2% vs. 1.8% respectively.

The lifetime rate of PTSD among adults was estimated to be 6.8% in the 2001 survey. The lifetime prevalence estimate is remarkably stable when compared with the results obtained from the first National Comorbidity Study done in the early 1990's. At the time of the earlier study, the lifetime risk of PTSD was calculated to be 7.8%. The variance may be an artifact of sample differences, only 15 to 54 year olds were eligible in the 1990 study whereas the sampling frame was expanded to adults 18 or over in 2001.

Translating the figures into numbers of people and assuming the population of adults 18 years or older in the US is about 230 million, roughly 8 million people currently have or have had PTSD in the past year, of which 6 million will be women and 2 million men, based on population estimates 118 Million and 112 Million respectively. With lifetime rates of PTSD in the 6.8% to 7.8% range, as many as 15.6 to 17.9 million adults will have PTSD at some point in their lives.

As a point of reference, following are prevalence rates, 12 month and lifetime, for several other common psychiatric disorders as measured by the 2001 National Comorbidity Survey.

	12 Month	Lifetime
PTSD	3.6%	6.8%
Panic Disorder	2.7%	4.7%
Obsessive-Compulsive Disorder	1.2%	2.3%
Bipolar Disorder	2.8%	4.4%
Alcohol Abuse	3.1%	13.2%

Only alcohol abuse, which is often paired with PTSD as a coping strategy, is more common than PTSD in the general population and then only on a lifetime basis. By any standard then PTSD is a major mental health problem.

Prevalence of PTSD is moreover much higher among subpopulations that are prime candidates for the disorder, e.g., combat veterans, violent crime victims, as one would expect. Nevertheless, PTSD is neither universal among those who are traumatized nor affects even a majority of them. A meta-analysis summarizing 24 studies involving a total of 2,383 heart attack survivors, for example, found only 12% will develop PTSD. Given that roughly 1 million people in the US survive a heart attack annually, PTSD still represents a significant medical problem affecting 120,000 people each year and because heart attack survivors who experience PTSD have nearly double the risk of subsequent medical complications including death.

It happens that the prevalence of PTSD among heart attack survivors is a good approximation for other high risk groups.

For instance, among male combat veterans of various wars the prevalence of PTSD is: Vietnam = 15.2%, Gulf War = 10.1%, Iraq = 13.8%. The estimates for earlier wars are harder to come by as the disorder was less likely to be recognized. Nonetheless one estimate for WWII combatants is 9% with a much higher rate among those engaged in more significant action, and 7% among Korean War veterans.

Other groups show similar rates: government workers who witnessed the World Trade Center attacks from nearby buildings, 9-10%, rape victims, 11% as examples. All of the groups mentioned above have lifetime rates of PTSD in the 20% to 30% range. The inescapable conclusion is: PTSD is manifest among a consistent minority of individuals who have experienced a life threatening trauma whether the source of the exposure is military, medical or criminal.

Brain Imaging

Advances in brain imaging over the past decade help to establish a physiological foundation for PTSD symptoms and behaviors and tie them to specific structures in the brain. Central among these is the amygdala a primitive structure located just above the brain stem in the temporal lobe. The amygdala is associated with an array of emotional responses to environmental stimuli, most relevant to PTSD being the "fight or flight" response to threat, processing of fear related stimuli and memory formation and storage.

The amygdala appears to be hyperactive and enlarged among those with PTSD and significantly, the amount of enlargement and increases in activity are correlated with increasing severity of PTSD symptoms. The relationship is suggestive vis-à-vis causal since as yet it has not been determined if the enlargement of the amygdala is a risk factor for PTSD, preceding exposure and predisposing some to acquire the disorder or if trauma associated with the life threat causes changes in the underlying structure of the brain. At issue is whether it is individual traits or characteristics of the traumatic event that generate PTSD symptoms.

Two other areas of the brain also appear to be involved in the incidence and expression of PTSD, the medial prefrontal cortex and the hippocampus. The former is particularly significant since it is associated with higher order cognitive tasks such as decision-making and problem-solving. Additionally the medial prefrontal cortex interacts with the amygdala in the processing and storage of memory, i.e., the conversion of short-term to long-term memory.

People with PTSD tend to have smaller or atrophied medial prefrontal cortexes when compared with controls, an observation that fits well with the reported impairment in decision-making those with PTSD, myself included, experience. Like the amygdala, the greater the abnormality in the medial prefrontal cortex, the more severe the PTSD symptoms, although in this case, the relationship is inverse.

The hippocampus is the odd man out in some respects as it seems to play an independent role in PTSD. Located in the temporal lobe near the amygdala, the hippocampus is involved in the formation of new memories and the conversion of short-term to long term memories as well as spatial perception and navigation that probably have little to do with PTSD. There is scant evidence to suggest that the hippocampus interacts with the other two structures in creating PTSD symptoms.

The hippocampus is instrumental in recall of memories possibly explaining the source of flashbacks and re-visiting phenomenon present among people with PTSD. Those with PTSD have smaller hippocampi than controls. Some twin studies, in which one identical twin was exposed to a traumatic event and the other not, however indicate that both twins have smaller hippocampi than normal suggesting a small hippocampus may predispose one to PTSD. Conversely, some studies of trauma patients suggest the hippocampus shrinks in response to the crisis.

The brain imaging studies, in sum, have been quite insightful providing as they do a physiological foundation for the cognitive and emotional reactions that are commonly associated with and help to define PTSD. What remains to be teased out is whether the cerebral markers observed in brain imaging studies predispose some individuals to acquire PTSD in the aftermath of trauma, an explanation that would fit well with the lack of universality of PTSD among trauma survivors, or if they result from PTSD itself. Another area of fruitful future brain imaging research will be to determine if therapies can alter the underlying cerebral structures to correct enlarged or atrophied structures, in short to demonstrate a cure for PTSD.

Manifestations

As one might imagine with such an expansive definition of an experience as emotionally fraught as PTSD discussions surrounding the disorder can be quite controversial. The debate frequently revolves around the question: Who owns PTSD? That is, who legitimately can be said to be suffering from it and who not. At stake is the perceived devaluating of the unique experience of one group by the inclusion of another.

PTSD has its origins in the recognition of the debilitating impact of combat on soldiers. Known as shell shock in WWI and combat fatigue in WWII, combat veterans have a primacy in their claim on the applicability of PTSD to their service. The name alone was instrumental in changing attitudes toward a disorder stigmatized and shamed initially as cowardice and shirking enabling it instead to be treated dispassionately as a disease. Soldiers have been put in a life threatening situation, often many times, occasions of extreme violence they have witnessed or taken part in. Many too have volunteered to fight for patriotic reasons. Thus including others in the fraternity of PTSD sufferers can be seen as diminishing the service of these individuals and the sacrifices made by them.

Rape victims meanwhile can feel that PTSD describes their mental status in the face of the heinous form of predation they experienced. Allowing someone like me, who qualifies for medical reasons, to use the label PTSD to describe their post trauma thoughts and actions devalues the experience of rape victims, some feel, by allowing the very personal violation that is rape to go unacknowledged.

There is a grain of truth to these distinctions and I am sympathetic to the argument in some regards. I never willingly put myself in danger. No one ever violated my body (well maybe one IV nurse who had trouble finding a vein, but not as a rule). My claim to the mantle of the PTSD stricken is solely a matter of misfortune. But the unique circumstances of the causal event do not confer a special status or solitary hold on the disease. What differentiates PTSD from other anxiety disorders is not only exposure to a life threatening event but as importantly, a set of characteristic and consistent aberrant thoughts, emotions and actions.

The common manifestations of PTSD have been organized into four categories in the Fifth Edition of the APA's Diagnostic and Statistical Manual (DMS-V), the authoritative reference and taxonomy of mental disorder; they include:

- **Re-experiencing** – e.g., spontaneous memories, flashbacks, recurrent dreams like the ones I experienced
- **Avoidance** – e.g., attempts to avoid distressing thoughts, emotions, places and other reminders of the event
- **Negative cognitions and mood** – e.g., estrangement from others, diminished interest in activities, excessive blaming of self or others – something that figured so prominently in my sense of victimization as described in the next chapter
- **Arousal** –e.g., hyper-vigilance, aggressive, reckless and self-destructive behavior – descriptive of my reactions to the Hospitalists and primary care physician's staff.

DMS-V is a reference for mental health professionals intended to insure some uniformity in diagnosis and treatment of mental disorders. For those of us who have struggled with PTSD though the symptoms come not in categories but in more pixilated form. There are dozens of individual expressions of PTSD that are subsumed under the DMS-V categories. I am sure like every other person with PTSD I had most of them at one time or another.

Earlier I related examples of my near nightly re-experiencing of the traumatic event through dread and dreams. A few examples from my experience that might fit the other DMS-V categories include the following.

Avoidance

I was encouraged after leaving the hospital to start exercising as soon practicable and to exercise to the limits of my capacity. Since almost all the things I liked to do were now hazardous and off limits, biking (falling risk), scuba diving (lung stress), kayaking and swimming (DVT aggravation), I was left with walking. I began the road back the day after I left the hospital not two weeks from the date of the attack on the beach. Walking to the end of the block, perhaps 200 yards, was the best I could do. Several days later I was up to two blocks, from my house to the ocean.

My wife often accompanied me on the walks in case I had another emergency. The first time we walked across the short boardwalk to the dunes, I started to turn right as I always did and walk along the shore. But there ahead, just a short way off was the blue-roofed building that marked the spot of the attack. When I saw it I stopped, hesitated, then turned around and walked in the other direction. It was just to "creepy" to go by the spot I explained to my wife. The memories were too fresh, the emotions too near the surface.

It would be weeks before I felt comfortable walking past the spot and months before I could pass the house without marking it mentally and acknowledging its significance. Confidence in the continuation of life does return, albeit slowly, however. A year later I pass the place without noticing or replaying the events that happened there.

Cognition

My cognitive abilities were quite obviously compromised post trauma. I was easily distracted and had difficulty staying on task or completing one if it required any significant concentration. Planning and decision-making were especially problematic. I had trouble focusing on the objective and deciding on a course of action. It was not a function of too little evaluation of options, quite the contrary I did too much.

I could not seem to stay on a straight path toward the objective but instead wondered into every side route or cul-de-sac to explore it. I considered so many alternatives I could not pull the trigger on any one of them without pausing to double check the others all over again. This kind of chasing-my-tail decision-making lead to a number of poor business and personal decisions in the months after the PE.

Ironically one of the best examples I have of the disturbance in my cognitive capacity I experienced came as a function of my effort to document the crisis and journey back to health in this book. While writing, disturbing memories and frightening thoughts would pop up at inopportune times to break a line of thought. I have been stopped midsentence and had trouble restarting, my mind a complete blank to my previous place. Even the simplest task like searching for a word that could not be recalled or lingering over a word choice brought me up short.

Not only was it difficult to focus on the work at hand but the journalistic activity worked in direct opposition to my recovery by forcing me to relive the experience and revisit the emotions it engendered. If recovery from PTSD is a matter of reestablishing defense mechanisms against the specter of sudden death, as suggested by the quote at the start of the chapter by Dr. Lickerman, himself a survivor of a massive and unprovoked PE, then trying to describe my experience in writing had exactly the opposite effect.

Mood

Emotionally I was on a roller coaster with dominant emotions such as depression, fear, anger, withdrawal, undulating through time like partially overlapping sine waves of feelings. Depression was the most pronounced in the early going when I was most restricted in what I could do and felt helpless and dependent. Later anger with myself and others would emerge as the dominant feeling taking precedence over the others. I distanced myself from friends and family, cutting off relationships built over a lifetime. The effort to maintain relationships was daunting and I tired very quickly of explaining myself and my condition.

The emotional tides were not stages per se and not as clear cut as I appear to make them. They did not flow from one to another in progression like the stages of grief experienced by terminally ill patients and described so masterfully by Dr. Elisabeth Kübler-Ross. Instead they were surges in emotion that waxed and waned throughout the recovery. In retrospect for me recognizing the tidal flow of feelings was a window to understand, and sometimes forgive, my labile behavior during those stressful early months.

At first I did not realize that I was the ball in the Pachinko machine bouncing from one emotional extreme to another. It was not until much later in the recovery process, when I started to research PTSD while writing this book in fact, that I became aware the turmoil I felt and often expressed inappropriately was not unique to my personality or experience but rather was a characteristic of the disorder. Before this realization my behavior was often inexplicable to me and at times the source of acute embarrassment.

Arousal

One of the curious things about the physical expression of PTSD was that my body had become a stranger to me. It was as if I were detached from it, something I did not know, an object removed from me that I inspected. My physical self was an entity I would need to become acquainted with all over again. In some respects it was a matter of trust. My body had let me down in the most fundamental way possible and I would have to learn to live with it again in peace, to feel safe that there would be no more surprises.

Oddly with this detachment from my body came an excessive awareness of it, hyper-vigilance with all things somatic. Every unexpected twinge or pain, and there were so very many in the early going, was cause for a mental MRI full body scan to make sure I was alright. Sharp pains would set off anxiety alarms especially if I was alone. I would lie on the couch with my leg elevated to promote blood flow all the while with my muscles clenched in dire anticipation of the next attack I was sure would come. I was perpetually on guard for the next PE, standing sentinel to sound the alarm and summon aid.

One somatic sequela in particular became something of a bellwether by which I measured the progress of my healing, a catch in my chest that appeared when I started to exercise shortly after leaving the hospital. It was a discontinuity in pulse and breathing that terrified me as if something was impeding blood from flowing smoothly into my lungs and locking my ribs together so I could not take a full breath. The first time I experienced it, I was prompted to do an immediate about face and retreat to the relative safety of my home. Fortunately it was predictable, localized to the same spot in my chest, coming at the same point in the walk and lasting only a few minutes. Eventually, after perhaps three months, it tapered off and finally ceased all together.

Superstitious Behavior

One of the odd after effects of my hyper-vigilance to physical cues was the development of superstitious behaviors. Normally superstition is thought of as beliefs or behaviors having a supernatural foundation, i.e., ritualized actions that will insure that some beneficial outcome occurs because an omnipotent power is gratified, perhaps amused, by them. Superstition is then the belief that two events not necessarily connected by time and action can be dependent and one a cause of the other if the ritual is repeated faithfully. In other words seeing a cause where one does not exist and holding to this belief in the absence of empirical evidence. It is the misattribution for why a particular event did or did not occur therefore, and of obtaining a propitious end through the rote replication of ritual.

I am referring more specifically to superstitious behavior as it is understood in an operant conditioning context. Operant conditioning is a simple but robust theory that says behavior is affected by the rewards or punishments that follow it. A behavior is more apt to occur in the future if it is followed by a reward, positive reinforcement, or if there are no negative consequences to it. Conversely, the same behavior will become less frequent over time if it is followed by punishment, negative reinforcement. This behavioral learning model has the attributes of all great theories; it is deceptively simple, seemingly obvious and genuinely profound in its implications and applications.

The system of rewards and punishments is most effective in shaping behavior if it is consistent, i.e., the same behavior elicits the same response, positive or negative, most of the time and if it closely follows the behavior so the relationship between the two is apparent. When rewards and punishments are inconsistent or delayed, intermittent as operant conditioners say, the effect of reinforcement is attenuated or strange things start to happen. Another kind of superstitious behavior emerges, an unthinking one with no supernatural imperative.

B.F. Skinner, the most prominent proponent of operant conditioning, used pigeons to demonstrate the principles. Birds were rewarded with a pellet of food if they pecked a bar that released it. Through trial and error pigeons found the lever, received reinforcement in the form of food and were quickly conditioned to peck the lever whenever they wanted more. Skinner also observed that when the release of the pellet was delayed or not provided in every case, the birds developed bizarre and ritualized behavior. They moved in tight circles always in the same direction, bobbed their heads to one side and back, pecked at nonexistent levers and so on. The behaviors were acquired through trial and error as before, but in this case they were paired with an inappropriate, noncausal behavior such that the actions became more exaggerated over time to account for the uncertainty of reward.

For me the operant conditioning model seems like an apt metaphor for some of the quirky behaviors I developed after the crisis. Take as an example my superstitious grasping of my wrist to take my pulse whenever I feel a heart flutter or momentary arrhythmia. I know how strange this must appear to other people so I try to do it surreptitiously. I attempt to delude myself into believing people don't notice, creating a fiction to preserve my self-esteem, but they no doubt do.

Then there is my unwillingness to go anywhere without having protection and a life line to aid. Going for a walk on the beach is inconceivable unless I carry along my cellphone, blood oxygen meter and Lovenox injector just in case. Forgetting one or both of these security blankets would send me into near panic in the months immediately following the event. Now I superstitiously carry them. I have become the equivalent of an anticoagulant junkie, hiding syringes of heparin in easy to reach places as if they were so many bottles of scotch or vials of pills.

I have carried the syringes so long without using them every one is past the expiration date on the package. No matter. Preventing or mitigating a new PE is not really their function any more. It is instead a prop to give me a sense of calm and well-being so I can carry on. Ironically, when it actually came time to administer a Lovenox injection in an emergency I forgot to do so. My second PE occurred early in the morning while walking to the bathroom. I made it back to the bed and sat waiting for the EMS ambulance to arrive. On the bed stand was a Lovenox injector ready to use, but I didn't have the presence of mind to recall it was there much less give myself a shot.

I do not pretend to believe these behaviors developed or in any way are perpetuated by the lack of adverse health consequences that follow them. I am not so addled as to think taking my pulse will ward off a heart attack or PE. The reinforcement I receive is more psychological than physical. It is not the avoidance of another event that makes me act strangely, it is the anticipation of one that does. More precisely, it is the lessening of emotions and preoccupations that provide the reinforcement that gives the actions life. When I faithfully follow the rituals there is a reduction in tension, anxiety and fear, replaced by feelings of well-being and safety. Among other things there is also the comfort that I have done all I can and I am absolved of any responsibility for whatever happens.

Superstitious behaviors are self-reinforcing and can be so tightly wound they become obsessive, unmoored from rational underpinnings. They are second-order motives once removed from a substrate of reality, ones where thoughts and feelings become the reason for the act, where avoiding the dread associated with anticipating an event rather than the event itself motivates. This is not, I suppose, all that different from any other phobic reaction. As a once fearful flyer I developed preflight rituals that were sure to keep the plane airworthy and myself calm. The superstitious choreography still accomplishes its function and I slavishly follow the ritual to this day. It is not the vanishingly small probability of an accident occurring but rather the anticipation of one before take-off that makes them indispensable.

Summary

Sadly, the possibility that I might be exhibiting signs of PTSD was never mentioned by any of my caregivers during treatment with one exception.

"Are you depressed?" the Internist asked one day out of the blue in the course of a routine follow-up visit.

"Yes." I replied simply after a moment's reflection.

Nothing followed. The dialogue ended there as abruptly as it started. The issue was dropped never to be raised again. Instead the physical causes, symptoms and sequelae of the disease were treated medically and chemically to the exclusion of any other options.

Barring that one brief question posed by my physician, the mental health dimensions of my condition and the need for mental health support was never broached while I convalesced nor has it ever been raised in the two years since the event. It was a glaring omission in an otherwise comprehensive treatment regimen, one that I, of necessity, attempted to rectify on my own.

Given the incidence of PTSD caused by sudden, traumatic medical problems and its impact on recovery from them, this was a significant missed opportunity to improve my rehabilitative care, I believe. Offering the opportunity for palliative care as a matter of course to those who have endured a life threatening medical problem or procedure could be an opportunity for the medical profession and mental health therapists to extend and improve the overall treatment of people who have suffered medical emergencies and their families.

TREATMENT AND RECOVERY

The Circle of Life

Recovery from a near death medical crisis was a protracted process that took considerable time and effort. Getting well became a full time occupation and preoccupation leaving little time for anything else. In the six months following the PE not a week would go by without at least one, sometimes two or three, follow-up visits with the specialists that treated some aspect of my disease and labs that measured my return to health. As part of my treatment I saw at regular intervals an:

- Internist
- Vascular Surgeon
- Hematologist
- Radiologist
- Pulmonologist

and after a major Coumadin related bleeding incident, an Ear, Nose and Throat specialist. (I always preferred the archaic nomenclature for that specialty Otorhinolaryngologist – say it fast, it will clear your sinuses). This in addition to my twice annual check-ups by a Dermatologist.

Interspersed between doctor appointments I saw a number of technicians, stopped at the pharmacy for prescription refills, and visited several labs that drew my blood, checked my INR, performed periodic ultrasounds, MRI's and pulmonary function tests. Any downtime was spent organizing a small library of medical records my treatment generated and trying to decipher the occult mysteries of medical billing.

Where I live in south Florida consulting with the medical profession has become the modern equivalent of the Circle of Life. Retirees do laps weekly on the chronic care circuit. Doctors no longer make rounds, patients do. Retirement villages and assisted living facilities run daily bus tours to doctors' offices where seniors are deposited to wile away their day staring blankly at the banks of TV monitors that blare a steady diet of Fox News propaganda on the evils of debt, the Constitutional glories of the Second Amendment and the perils of socialized medicine, which not coincidentally is about to pay for their visit.

Afternoons are devoted to exercise. This consists of the retirement home bus dropping the ambulatory seniors at the nearest Publix supermarket where they wander slowly – very slowly – through the store. Many lean on their shopping carts using them as rolling walkers, their chests resting on arms and elbows splayed out on the handlebar, frequently dragging an oxygen cylinder behind. From above it must look like an amusement park for the aged where the elderly try to negotiate the aisles in something akin to a super slow motion demolition derby.

Monday morning at the blood lab is like old home week. All the patients are regulars who know everyone else there. A bizarre circadian rhythm insures they will all arrive with the unlocking of the lab door and by 7:05AM the waiting room is crowded and the wait is estimated to be one hour. Nevertheless waiting time is productively spent catching up on all the news of neighbors and friends. Who was not in church the day before and why – usually a hospitalization, more rarely a death? Who was due for surgery? Who had improved? Who had worsened?

I hated to admit to myself that I too had become a regular on the Circle of Life merry-go-round, waiting to grasp for the brass ring of medicinal goodies as they passed by. But I adapted. I learned to visit Publix in the morning and the blood lab in the afternoon to avoid the rush but this was small accommodation to the rhythms of chronic care Circle of Life. Hakuna Matata.

The Pharmacalization of Society

One of the most disconcerting aspects of the recovery was coming to terms with the fact that I might be chronically ill. It took me a considerable amount of time to come to this realization and even longer to admit to myself that it might be true. I assumed that I would bounce back in short order to my pre-attack health status. But as time went on my posse of specialists began to dissuade me of this fantasy, dangling the carrot of my cure farther ahead and always just out of my reach.

Coumadin was the symbolic yardstick of my recovery. I was cured when I could stop taking it – simple enough. Originally a three month regimen was prescribed. It was extended to six months because of the size of the PE and eventually, after a full body scan and battery of genetic tests, to a year "just to be safe" because the PE was "unprovoked" that is, had no identifiable cause. However after a second PE occurred when I briefly stopped taking Coumadin it was clear I would be a Coumadin "lifer".

I was reminded each morning over breakfast that something fundamental had changed in my life. There before me in addition to a bowl of oatmeal and the New York Times was a 7 day pill organizer filled with the recommended daily allowance of Coumadin. Being tethered to a drug for my continued existence made me at once frustrated, angry and depressed. The fact that I needed a pill organizer, an iconic emblem of old age in my opinion, to make sure I would not forget my daily dose did nothing but add salt to a self-inflicted wound.

I was in my early 60's and up until this point had lead, outside of a daily 81mg aspirin, a largely drug free existence. In fact, I prided myself on not being medicated for any chronic disease. It was an endless source of disbelief and awe among medical professionals I consulted, not to mention an opportunity for smug self-satisfaction on my part, that I took no drugs regularly, **at my age**.

I am not one who takes drugs indiscriminately and never without careful consideration of the consequences. My long held belief is most Americans are overmedicated and the focus of many drugs is intended to forestall aging and the entropy of decrepitude as if somehow the second law of thermodynamics could be suspended in the case of personal health. Or they are aimed at inconveniences that can be ameliorated by natural processes, sleep comes to mind, or if not, can be tolerated.

Have you ever noticed how difficult it is to leave a doctor's office without a prescription for some pharmaceutical product? The prescription has become the symbolic representation for the doctor that the consultation has been concluded successfully· Treatment was delivered. No matter how often I tell a physician I will not take a recommended drug or fill the prescription I have just been given the pressure to do so is unrelenting. I find it is easier to accept the script and discard it on the way out of the office than it is to engage the provider in a debate over the merits of the drug or my intentions to use it or not.

One post hospitalization follow-up visit I had is illustrative. I complained of shortness of breath (dyspnea) not a particularly startling after effect of a PE. The nurse asked if I used oxygen. No? Did I want to? No thanks? How about a respirator? No again—I must be a hard case. She then suggested a prescription for bronchodilators "just in case I needed it." I was adamant; I did not want it, would not fill it and had no intention of using the drug. But in the face of implacable insistence I took the script just to end the appointment. On my next visit to an unrelated specialist, my record reflected that I was taking a bronchodilator and used a respirator for dyspnea. I have lost insurance coverage over less.

I am not by any means disputing the value of these therapies for people who need them. My company was responsible for the analysis of many of the clinical trials that lead to the original approval of bronchodilators by the FDA. I've seen the evidence—they work. I am disputing the need to prescribe something for every patient on every visit so the provider feels they have performed their function to treat.

Other trends provide further tail winds for the increased use of pharmaceuticals, especially when a person reaches late middle age as I have. Many drugs now in use are designed to treat a chronic disease that over time will cause other more serious diseases, high blood pressure causing strokes or high cholesterol linked to a heart attack being prime examples. The function of the prescription and treatment regimen is primarily preventative therefore.

As a public health trained professional I understand the rationale behind this quite well. A basic tenet of public health is encapsulated in what is known as the prevention paradox.

> More cases of a disease will occur as a result of a population being at low risk for a disease than a small segment of the population being at a high risk.

The prevention paradox is public health 101, an observation containing all the hallmarks that distinguish the discipline of public health from the practice of medicine: focus on populations vs. individuals, prevention vs. treatment, and quantification in terms of risks vs. cases. The benefits of this perspective are incontrovertible and as a public health person, I am a true believer.

Take high blood pressure, a.k.a. hypertension, as an illustration. The paradox predicts that if the **average** blood pressure of the **general population** is decreased by some amount, say 10 points of systolic pressure and 5 points of diastolic, a greater number of cases of hypertension and hypertension-caused strokes will be prevented, than if individuals with high blood pressure, let's say above 140 systolic and 100 diastolic pressures, were treated. This relationship continues down the blood pressure scale. The greater the reduction in the average population pressures the fewer hypertension-related diseases there will be.

It is almost impossible to argue with the logic. The statistics are too compelling. It applies equally well to other measures that are harbingers of chronic disease such as high cholesterol. So anti-hypertensives are prescribed by the freight car load, statins by the billions. The American public is better off and healthier because of it. But there is also no denying that a perfect synergy has been created between the need, real and psychological, for physicians to treat disease, the corporate imperatives to sell product and the inexhaustible willingness of the public to spend in order to preserve health and increase longevity.

The synergy takes on a momentum of its own and it can spawn unintended consequences. Chief among these is disease-creep. When I was young it was accepted lore among practitioners that blood pressure and with it the definition of hypertension changed with age. The rule of thumb was an acceptable systolic blood pressure was 100 plus your age. So for a person my age a systolic blood pressure of 160 was perfectly acceptable. Today 140 over 90 is considered uncontrolled hypertension and the point at which antihypertensive drugs are prescribed if not before. Now imagine how many cases of stroke could be prevented if hypertension were defined as 130 over 85. Why stop there? The prevention logic still holds if the definition is lowered to 120 over 80 and beyond.

It does not take long before disease-creep leads to the classification of most adults as hypertensive—in other words, sick. Another powerful economic driver is created. The more people who are diagnosed with the disease, the more physician visits will be generated to monitor and manage the cases and the more drugs that will be prescribed and sold. The economics are especially favorable for a chronic disease where a person is treated "for life."

Consumers, now patients, benefit as well—at least in the aggregate cases of hypertension-caused disease decline when summed across the entire population. But will a specific individual benefit? Only to the degree that the risk in the general population is reduced. As an example, if two out of three people who have hypertension have a stroke (I do not pretend these figures are anything other than heuristic) and those odds decline to one-in-three if everyone in the population with hypertension is treated, then it is clearly in a person's favor to play the odds and get treatment. But the odds are still one-in-three they will experience a stroke despite being treated. More importantly, there is no way to predict *ceretis paribus* if they will be among the unfortunate third. It is not possible to predict individual outcomes from population level statistics, in other words. Conversely, there is no way to negate the population benefit or that it increases the more universal treatment is with individual exceptions.

Another unintended consequence of the prevention paradox is the subtle trend toward a pharmacalized society. The greater the percentage of the population who are "sick", the more diseases each of us has, the more apt we all are to seek medical and chemical solutions. In the case of chronic diseases there simply are no solutions—in the long term we are all dead of something. More problematic are ailments that retard natural processes, e.g. aging, or ones whose principle symptoms are inconveniences that can be addressed with lifestyle changes or just letting nature run its course, e.g. antibiotics do not cure viral infections, time does.

Then there is the problem of iatrogenic disease, ones where the treatment for one disease causes another, often more serious one. It is impossible to watch primetime television without coming across iatrogenic pharmaceuticals multiple times throughout the night. Listen to the side effects of products for erectile fatigue, insomnia, depression, smoking cessation, love handles, and my personal favorite restless leg syndrome (itself possibly caused by drugs for other ailments). Is treating these diseases worth the risk of suicidal ideation, major organ failure or sudden death? Personally I'll take dancing feet any day over the risk of sudden death—been there, done that. Maybe I'm just an inveterate curmudgeon. I wonder if there is a drug for that.

Mantras and Meditation

Despite the appointments, tests, and prescriptions, the medical profession proved to be unable or unwilling to address the emotional side of my illness, the mental turmoil that characterized the aftermath of my brush with sudden death. I was referred to every other specialty that was remotely relevant to the treatment of my condition, but never a practitioner specializing in mental health, whether it be a psychiatrist, psychologist, social worker or pastoral counselor. Knowing only vaguely what PTSD was and not imaging I could be suffering with it I did not have the presence of mind to ask for a referral.

I found myself alone to solve the problem without access to professional resources that could help. I could not turn to my family for the counseling I needed. They were as clueless as I was about what was going on. Besides they were neither objective nor trained to handle the task and they were going through their own reaction to my sudden demonstration of mortality, chronic illness and protracted recovery. They were facing an adjustment as emotionally difficult as my own. PTSD is nothing if not a family disease.

Not knowing what was wrong, I did not know how to fix it. Eventually I found my way to a friend and gifted therapist who helped me understand and cope with the emotional deluge. Other times I resorted to home remedies. Mantras and meditation were prime examples.

Mantras are white noise machines for the psyche. They drown out a cacophony of unpleasant thoughts with soothing sounds, pithy aphorisms and repetition. They steel the resolve to carry on when running away, cowering or uncontrolled blubbering seem preferable.

Afraid? The 23rd Psalm is comforting to repeat

> *Yea, though I walk through the shadow of death*
> *I shall fear no evil, for thou art with me.*
>   (King James Version)

Thoughts of death got you paralyzed? Put them out of your mind by intoning Caesar's fatalistic homily

> *Cowards die many times before their death*
> *The valiant never taste of death but once*
> *Of all the wonders I yet have heard*
> *It seems most strange to me that men should fear*
> *Seeing that death, a necessary end*
> *Will come when it will come*
>   (Julius Caesar, Act 1, Scene 2)

For stability when the world is little but disorder, the alcoholic's prayer can't be beat

> *God, grant me the serenity*
> *To accept the things I cannot change*
> *The courage to change the things I can*
> *And the wisdom to know the difference*

Buddhists seem to have taken the use of mantras to the level of high art. Ohm mani padre hum – roughly translated "Behold the jewel in the lotus." It doesn't do much for me but its power is evident in myriad carved stones that decorate hillsides along Himalayan paths and prayer flags that festoon mountain passes. I suspect the power of ohm mani padre hum derives as much from being chanted continuously in basso monotone as the spiritual message it conveys. Truly white noise.

Mantras are anticipatory, part of the coping arsenal I carry, ready to be hauled out in the right circumstance. They are no doubt valuable when extreme conditions are encountered and staying put is not an option. Being somewhat cowardly I've used mantras for years, decades before the PE. I still do. But they are like the paper lunch bags one blows into to stifle an anxiety attack or a safe word to flee to. What I needed after the PE was a means to lasting stress relief and comfort, one that could provide a cognitive transformation not just a firewall against bad thoughts. My fears, anxieties and preoccupations were chronic not transitory. Meditation appeared to provide promise.

I did not make a thorough study of meditation during my recovery nor did I intend to. My goal was much more utilitarian, to be a practitioner, to see if meditation "worked" for me to keep the brains banshees away. But meditation had a way of frustrating me. I had heard about the benefits of meditation for years and had dabbled with its practice on and off. As much as I tried I couldn't shake the feeling that I just wasn't doing it right. There were no visions, no calming or stress relieving benefits I could discern. My mind often wandered while attempting to meditate so I found myself continually hitting the reset button on the meditation tape, starting over only to lose my way again. I couldn't seem to train my mind to empty and prevent it from wandering to other topics.

I decided to use my first trek in the Himalayas as an opportunity to explore meditation in greater depth, learning from those who were experienced in the technique. I sat with my guide on the banks of the Kali Gandaki River in lotus position, and chanted Ohmmm... not an easy feat given the sharp, fist-sized rocks strewn about. This was even worse than trying to meditate alone. So we worked on breathing, in on the Ohm, out on the Mani Padre Hum. Again no luck.

Examples of devotion to meditation surrounded me everywhere I looked. Carved stones, prayer flags, and in one place a mani wall nearly a mile long, built of stones, painted the seven colors Buddhists favor and containing within it hundreds of prayer wheels waiting to be turned by travelers passing across the barren Tibetan plateau. No matter how hard I tried though I could not make the magic work. In the midst of such an outpouring of faith, I rationalized my failure, attributing the pervasiveness of mediation by locals to their consumption of the psychotropic foliage that grew in abundance, like the acres of marijuana through which we walked and the poppies that decorated the borders of walkways to village houses.

Despite my lack of success I decided to delve into the meditation mystery again on my second trip to the Himalayas. This time I was able to secure a private audience with the head Lama of the Swayambhunath or as it is better known, the Monkey Temple in Kathmandu. Head of what is reputed to be the oldest stupa in the world dating to 200 BC, the Lama is a player in Buddhist circles. Yet he was completely unassuming, dressed so modestly as to be unrecognizable as a religious leader. We went to his private quarters, really a single room with a cot, where we drank the tea he made. We talked about his life and past lives. How he became a monk at 8, he was 45 when I met him. He was a woman in his previous life, he said, before being reincarnated as a man this go round.

Our conversation eventually found its way to meditation and karma. I told him I had tried to meditate but had trouble keeping the thoughts of the day from intruding. I was unable to empty my mind. He likened this to having things scattered around that need to be collected and put in a bubble (box) and once sealed I would experience the benefits of meditation. Apparently I appeared confused because he returned to the topic twice more to help me. He next compared meditation to a beehive. The bees leave the hive during the day but returned at night to gather around the queen.

Then he admonished me not to try too hard because it would cause stress and sicken my heart but just practice, practice, practice—the way to Carnegie Hall through meditation apparently. Finally he said it was like trying to count the stars—if you try to count them all you will fail and be frustrated but if you concentrate on a small part of the sky it is possible.

It was teaching by analogy, Buddhical parables. Unfortunately I found parables are not a good learning style for my cognitive disposition. I think I would prefer being graded on performance or enrolled in the meditation version of a ballet school where deviations from perfection are corrected in real time. So I continued to play at meditation until the PE when I truly needed the stress relief and preoccupation barrier it was reputed to provide.

The scientific evidence is beginning to accumulate that meditation does in fact help people deal with stress, anxiety, depression, intrusive thoughts, etc. In other words, all the kinds of symptoms I experienced after the vascular accident and more generally PTSD. Particularly exciting are studies that suggest the amygdala is structurally changed when people practice mediation since it plays such a central role in the manifestations of PTSD. Researchers, using MRI scans of the brains of meditating subjects are therefore on the verge of establishing a physiological basis for the reported effects of meditation and its utility for PTSD therapy.

The in-vogue style meditation of the day is "mindfulness." A Buddhist notion, mindfulness is a state in which one is aware of the here and now and is able to regard it in a dispassionate, nonjudgmental manner. Usually the process is started by concentrating on an environmental cue, most often breathing. Concentrating may be too aggressive a term. It is more the act of being aware of one's breathing. One returns to the cue whenever the mind wanders. I was pleased to learn this since it meant I wasn't "failing" when I tried to meditate in the past.

One of the practical benefits of mindfulness is its self-referential property. Being aware of oneself in the moment diverts the mind from the preoccupations and fears of the future, such as one's own mortality, something I often grappled with during the months that followed my brush with sudden death. It leaves little room for intrusive thoughts or perhaps more accurately it offers a means to refocus when they do intrude.

In this regard one can understand why mindfulness meditation can be effective in lessening the symptoms of obsessive-compulsive behavior disorders, e.g. stress, anxiety, fear, depression, ritualized behavior, all the emotions that dominated my recovery immediately post PE, in other words. Since in my mind if PTSD was not a traumatically acquired obsessive-compulsive disorder it was pretty close, so mindfulness mediation should help. I tried it again, regularly, and this time as the Lama recommended – not too hard.

I am not trying to sell Zen weekends in the Catskills, but for me meditation has been useful. However imperfectly I may practice it, meditation provides a welcome tool to help manage my emotional ups and downs. The calming effect is immediate and real, diverting my mind, allowing me to stop emotions and worries that might otherwise spiral out of control. I suspect there is much more to meditation than I have discovered so meditation remains a work in progress all the same.

Getting Better

I learned about PTSD ironically enough as the symptoms of it began to disappear. It was only apparent in retrospect what behaviors and mental processes made up PTSD when a symptom ceased as I gradually returned to a modicum of normalcy, an example being when the nightmares that caused me to dread sleep tapered off and finally ended. Over time I was able to recognize the cluster of cognitive, behavioral and social adaptations and adjustments that were precipitated by the vascular accident. I even began to gauge the progress of my recovery by how many symptoms had been shed.

My experience was PTSD not only tended to diminish and resolve over time but it did not reoccur with such virulence when I had a second PE some months later. Afterward I had fewer of the classic PTSD symptoms. Part of this I attribute to the searching I went through after the first event, the feelings, questions and concerns that preoccupied me then such as, victimization, mortality, faith, what and who I cherished, etc., and the answers I had already arrived at. The disease pattern followed a similar progression as well so I knew what to expect and that whatever the manifestation was, I knew it would diminish and disappear with time.

When exercising, I had the same catch in my chest, the irregularity in pulse and hitch while taking in a breath, as I did during the first recovery. It was scary then but disappeared after a month or two. After the second PE it was there again but my attitude toward it had changed. I knew it for what it was, when it would occur, e.g., how far into a walk, and that it represented no imminent threat. Like the first abnormality it disappeared on its own. There were new symptoms to be sure but I was much more likely to accept them at face value. I took them as indications I was healing, not that I was about to die.

At some point along the way I stopped trying not to die and started trying to live. It was as if I turned a corner where my thoughts and actions were less about how to avoid another life ending event. I began to think of the future and the prospect that the life ahead might be long after all and was worth living however long it would prove to be. It would not be the same carefree life I had before exactly, when it was possible to suspend belief in my own mortality. Death would happen someday I knew but I could again persuade myself the day was far off.

CHAPTER FOUR
VICTIMIZATION—FATE
AND FORGIVENESS

"Are doctors who make mistakes villains? No, because then we all are."

—*Atul Gawande, M.D.*

(1965-)

A hospital stay is stultifyingly boring, ennui punctuated by brief flurries of activity, needle pokes, blood pressure cuffs, stethoscopes, medicine deliveries, and three squares a day of unseasoned yet surprisingly good food. In between, there was nothing for the idle mind, something my mother warned me repeatedly was the devil's workshop, to concentrate on other than the ire-inspiring question, why me?

Mistakes

Even before leaving the hospital I began to ruminate on my condition and how it came to be. As I replayed the tape countless times I became preoccupied with the part my primary care physician played in the way the events unfolded. I had a routine checkup with him just a few months before the vascular accident occurred. At the time all the classic signs of an active DVT were readily apparent. The leg below the knee was inflamed, warm to the touch and red in color. The calf was taut and swollen, painful when I walked or bent my knee. I found I could not sit for even an hour, in a play or a movie as an example, because of the severity and persistence of the pain.

I was convinced the leg needed attention and I suspected a DVT was present. During the exam, I recall pointing out the condition of my leg to the physician and expressing my concern that the symptoms could be caused by a blood clot. He examined the leg. Passed his hand over the shin to feel the warmth. He palpated the calf and used a tape measure to compare its size to the opposite leg – it was an inch larger in circumference.

All the while I piled on complaints rattling off a litany of symptoms, the chronic pain, the inability to sit for long periods and so forth, to flesh out the severity of the condition and to paint it in the worst light possible. It was my way of stacking the deck. If anything was seriously wrong, I reasoned, the doctor would pick up on it and prescribe a course of action to diagnosis and treat what was going on. If not, I would be reassured I was imagining problems.

In the end nothing happened. I recall leaving the appointment relieved in a sense because no specific malady was identified, in particular a DVT, but dissatisfied equally because something was clearly wrong. If it wasn't a DVT, what was it? No opinion was offered as to what it might be or how it could be diagnosed and treated. A routine noninvasive test, an ultrasound, could have resolved the matter quickly and unambiguously. It would have revealed large and dangerous clots in my leg and prompted immediate anticoagulation therapy. There would have been a subsequent hospital stay certainly but I would have avoided the pulmonary embolism. My flirtation with sudden death a few months later and all the grinding recovery and permanent physical injury I ultimately experienced never would have happened.

Inexplicably, and indefensibly in my view, the ultrasound was not ordered. There was, in effect, no downside to ordering the test. Yes, it would have cost some money, money that given my insurance deductible I would have to pay out-of-pocket. As far as I was concerned it was a price well worth paying to determine once and for all whether there was a problem and immediate treatment was indicated. For some reason the physician did not order it. More puzzling still, for some reason I did not demand it.

My thoughts were as always influenced by what happened to my mother. Since her death I was inordinately afraid of developing a DVT and dying suddenly of a pulmonary embolism. Never mind that she had classic risk factors for an acute DVT and subsequent PE, cancer, recent surgery, and immobility, none of which I had. Following her death my concern blossomed over time into a full-fledged phobia. I was as a result always alert for signs of an incipient problem and never failed to discuss my fears with my primary care physician if I had even the smallest indication of their accuracy. To add insult to injury I followed this routine for years since my mother's death. In fact, I had a similar examination several years earlier with a different primary care physician I had at the time. He didn't hesitate to order an ultrasound on the basis of far less extreme clinical indications.

If that had been the first time the leg was examined by my current physician treating the symptoms conservatively might have been understandable. But it was the second time in less than six months that I presented the same complaint and symptoms in an office visit and pointed them out to the physician for special attention. In the interim the condition had not resolved. By the second visit, it was obviously a chronic condition and warranted further exploration it seemed to me.

Even this I probably could have excused. What I could never reconcile was the office visit on Monday after the event. During the examination I was literally gasping for breath while at rest. The pants were far more extreme than anything I ever experienced after an hour on a treadmill. The doctor measured the oxygen saturation in my blood. It was 97%. He listened to my chest. It was clear. On the basis of those clinical findings he scheduled an ultrasound two days hence. Given my history, my description of the event, and the symptoms I presented the diagnosis should not have been difficult. I had suffered a pulmonary embolism. An immediate trip to the hospital was called for. More than any other aspect of the care and immediate post event treatment I received for my vascular accident this failure to intervene aggressively, while I was still very much in danger, stuck in my craw.

As I lay in the hospital the chain of missteps that put me there played on an endless loop in my mind. In the immediate aftermath of admittance to the hospital I was too sick, too scared and frankly too superstitious to let my suspicions blossom into a bouquet of anger. I was more mystified than angry. As the days slowly passed and it became clear I would survive a very close call my mind had freer range to contemplate the obvious errors that had, without my knowledge, nearly conspired to take my life. I became convinced I was the victim of a series of egregious medical mistakes.

Still questioning the judgment and competence of your primary physician is not something to be done lightly. The patient has a vested interest and strong motivation to believe in the doctor. You want them to be right if for no other reason than you want to know you are safe and will be well cared for. While in the throes of the controlled chaos a medical crisis is, it is not the right time to consider the possibility that a person you trust with your life is not performing adequately. The thought is just too terrifying, the cognitive dissonance too debilitating.

Malpractice

Nevertheless, even before leaving the hospital, the label "malpractice" reared its head. There certainly were, I was sure, causes of action – medical mistakes and damages – if I chose to push it. I even mentioned the possibility to my wife, voicing my belief that I could pursue the matter legally if I wanted. It was not an option I seriously entertained at that point, it was offered as a point of fact not as an intention to act. I was much more concerned with getting better and resuming my old life as soon as possible. Getting revenge, punishing the physician or seeking financial compensation was not the issue, climbing Mt. Kailash was.

Thoughts of malpractice ebbed and flowed during the recovery period nonetheless. I could not shake them. Before leaving the hospital I had to know for sure if my suspicions were accurate. I sought out confirmation therefore from every authoritative source that came my way, specialists of every stripe, that I was correct. At the end of one consultation with a specialist the day before I was released, I asked the attending nurse to leave the room while I spoke to the doctor in private.

When we were alone I asked him in an imploring way, "Were the symptoms I had before the event classic signs of a DVT?" I got an affirmative answer to this question no matter who I asked. The specialist being interrogated was no exception.

I followed with, "When I had the attack on the beach it was obviously a PE, wasn't it?" Again he gave an affirmative response.

"Don't you think my physician should have been able to recognize the DVT before the attack?" I pressed.

"Shouldn't he have known I had had a PE when I came to his office?"

These were the questions no doctor would answer. It called on them to critique a fellow professional, to break ranks and act as a judge of a peer's professional conduct. Usually the response I got was averted eyes, a shoulder shrug or some protestation that there was no way to tell. The closest anyone came to censure was a statement by one physician. "If it walks like a duck..." he said, his voice trailing off as he turned his palms upward.

It didn't matter. Failure to answer was tantamount to agreement. It was confirmation, if I ever really needed any, that a series of medical errors had been made. It verified that all the disruption of my life and the narrowed parameters I would have to live within going forward could have been avoided. At the same time it validated my sense of victimhood and justified my feelings of outrage that I had been singled out like this. It was permission to blame.

I could tell even at the time that the feelings welling up in me were very unhealthy. I could feel the anger rise, feel myself flush, my muscles tighten, my pulse quicken. I could hear it in my breathing, see it in my vital signs. For a person who always needed to be in control, I was helpless to affect anything. Concentrating on the what-might-have-beens did nothing but fuel the anger that showed every indication of boiling over into rage. At times, with physical effort it seemed, I had to redirect my thoughts to the positive side of my condition. It was no more complicated than I was alive. If I was a victim of fate, I was also on the right side of the coin toss when it mattered most.

I left the hospital thinly balanced between the joy of knowing I would live a while longer and the need to blame someone for nearly truncating what life I had left. I wanted an explanation other than unfeeling fate to explain why I was in the place I now found myself, to find a cause and effect which had they been different I never would have reached this state. I had found mine, it was a doctor who had made a chain of errors, whose medical judgment had been poor repeatedly and I had to pay the price for his incompetence. It's a short path from blame to seeking retribution and revenge and I was well down it.

So in the midst of this malignant brooding, it may seem incongruous that I returned to the care of the physician who I blamed with putting me there, but I did. I toyed with the idea of finding another physician to manage my post hospitalization recovery. But I soon realized that this option was nothing more than impotently spiteful and counterproductive. It would take time and energy, energy I did not have, to find another physician to supervise my recovery. Even if I could find someone suitable, I would have to make an effort to bring the new doctor up to speed on my medical history and present situation with no guarantee the replacement would be a better clinician than the one I had now. It was not a time to doctor shop I decided.

Besides, my doctor **owed me**. He had to be sweating my case. He knew he was wrong. I was **entitled** therefore to his full attention not to mention special consideration.

With expectations like these I was destined to be dissatisfied. When the care from the doctor or his office came up short by my assessment, it just added logs to the bonfire of resentment that had been kindled. What I failed to appreciate was the physician was operating in a highly structured, routinized even, milieu of prioritizing, allocating and dispensing care not of his making. For me a patient with fear-driven demands for information and carrying an outsized chip on my shoulder, the way medicine was practiced was galling and the physician was its face. I blamed my chosen scapegoat, the doctor for all the inadequacies I observed.

Even if my primary care physician wanted to perform the communication function I felt I needed it would have been difficult. He was protected by layers of bureaucratic barriers, as impenetrable as a medieval castle with an array of obstructions to prevent unwanted entry. A call center staffed by receptionists servicing the needs of 1,100 local physicians was the first line of defense, followed by triage nurses, nurse practitioners, scheduling clerks and so on. These people relayed my questions to the doctor and funneled back answers to me in a medical version of the child's game of telephone. In the oft chance that the physician received the right query and provided an answer, it was typically curt, instructional and one-dimensional. Like a Presidential press conference there was no opportunity for follow-on questions that could flesh out the response, provide the context within which it was made, or to describe the pros and cons of the other options that were considered.

In the best of cases the communication was incomplete and unsatisfying. In the worst, the physician's pique and exasperation at being bothered was palpable in the response. Demanding to speak with the doctor directly was the nuclear option, the method of last resort, reserved only for cases where complex conversation was required. This option was not to be engaged in lightly since one can get a reputation as a problem patient to be avoided at all cost. The penalty was banishment to a soundproof booth where communication with the office was delayed or not forthcoming or even permanent exile when the patient was "dropped", abandoned to find their way through the medical wilderness alone.

The health care zeitgeist created a system where the physician's time is a precious resource to be stored, hoarded, rationed and doled out begrudgingly. Patients become an annoyance, a necessary, albeit unpleasant, nuisance. The message is clear – the doctor's time is more valuable than the patient's peace of mind. The physician is a scarce resource, a precious metal that has been honed and fashioned into a disease-killing weapon. Of course, the firewalls physicians construct around themselves are not new. I remember my father, a General Practitioner in rural Michigan, having his receptionist or nurse deal with a difficult patient while he took refuge in the examining room. And like physicians today he was treated as a semi-godlike figure. The opportunity to avoid patients has been always been used, it has simply been institutionalized and industrialized now.

Is it not surprising then, that I prefaced each call I receive from my physician with an apology for "bothering" him? Why did I feel that, like everyone else, I needed to protect this individual – from myself no less?

The delays, willful or structural, lead to some spectacular blow-ups with the physician's office personnel especially if I detected the least bit of withholding. My paranoid state interpreted these instances as passive-aggressive. Of particular irritation were occasions when I would have my INR checked in a lab and the results were communicated to the doctor for "interpretation." I would have to wait for the lab to send the results to the physician's office, for the nurse to convey the results to the physician, for the physician to interpret the lab values, for the doctor to give orders for any change in dosage if needed and when to have the next blood test to the nurse, and for her to call me with the results and instructions. If I was not available to take the call, the nurse would not leave the INR reading on my answering machine for privacy reasons. I would have to call her back precipitating another trip through the surreal labyrinth known as the call center. If she was "with a patient" I would have to leave a message requesting a follow up call and the game of telephone tag would continue with the nurse now "it". Really was all this necessary? I was quite capable of understanding the meaning if the INR result was between 2 and 3 or not.

In the weeks immediately following the event the memory of trying to suck air into a nonworking collapsed lung was fresh and raw. So was the realization of how close I had come to death; I didn't have to grasp it mentally, I could feel it viscerally when I took a partial breath as the implications of my impaired breathing seeped into my awareness. Preventing another occurrence was the sole focus of my life. The INR readings took on disproportionate symbolic significance as a consequence. When the nurse called, left a message but not the INR value I was enraged. I focused on one nurse in particular who I was convinced was withholding information deliberately.

The penultimate point was reached when I was traveling to New York about six weeks after the attack. I made sure to carry Coumadin in my briefcase so I would not miss a dose on the off chance the airlines lost my luggage. Instead I did. I left the briefcase on the seat of the taxi as I exited upon reaching the destination. Everything was gone, not just my Coumadin but my last resort Lovenox syringes as well. I was pharmaceutically naked, medically out of touch and scared shitless.

I got to the room and began to frantically call any remotely relevant authority I could think of to track down the cabbie -- the taxi commission, the police, the Central Park - Park Service among others. While in the midst of the search, I called the doctor's office in Florida to get the INR results from the test I had that morning before leaving and to get new Coumadin prescriptions called into a local Manhattan pharmacy. I got a call back, but as usual the message gave no useful information, no INR values, no effort to make arrangements for a prescription that could be filled nearby. It was just a message that my call had been returned delivered in the voice of the nurse on whom I had focused my anger. I was livid. I called the office, got the call center and was informed that the office was closed for the day. That sent me into fear-driven harangue that lasted several minutes. I was shouting. I was completely out of control—hysterical. Then I felt justified, now I am ashamed with the way I acted.

That was the low point in my relationship with the doctor and his staff. He called the next day and told me in an avuncular way to "be nice" to the nurses because they were just doing their job. I, in turn, told him he needed to know what it was like to deal with his office. To his credit he heard me out without interrupting. Each of us having said our piece, we ended the call with an uneasy truce.

I remained suspicious of the office personnel however. Moreover the call reinforced in my mind that the physician was aware he had made an egregious mistake in the way he treated me before hospitalization but would not admit it. Why would he put up with my extreme behavior otherwise? How outrageous would I have to act before it set off a confrontation? The more the doctor put up with my antics the more it convinced me he knew he had something to hide. Twisted logic was the order of the day.

I waited to see if anything would change. It did not. Communication remained episodic and incomplete. Thoughts of revenge resurfaced with every delay encountered as I thought about how I was being treated. Shabbily was my conclusion. Without the deference due someone who was in this position because of someone else's mistake. My tolerance reached the breaking point one day when I sent in a question to the doctor through the telephone chain. The answer, when it came back, was conveyed to me by the nurse in a way that left no mistake that the doctor was fed up with my questions. The response was nothing short of snide, I believed. I decided to exercise the nuclear option. I demanded the physician call me so I could get answers to my question without interpretation by intermediaries.

Then I waited. There was no return call. I fumed. Two days went by. No call. A third day passed without contact. I'd had it. I began to explore legal options to see if I had cause to bring a malpractice suit. I called one of the nationwide ambulance chaser firms, one with a huge media budget and a website with a name something akin to www.youdeservejustice.com or maybe www.getthebastard.com. When a person answered I had one of those, this could only happen in America moments. It was another call center. The person on the other end was performing legal triage. After he took the facts of my potential claim he excused himself to talk with his supervisor. The supervisor was up next, he told me I appeared to have a case and I would hear from an attorney in a day or two. It was the legal mirror image of medical care system, the perverse reflection of medical practice as legal malpractice practice.

Another day passed. The physician did not call but the attorney did. I restated my case. The attorney responded that I had a cause for action if I wanted to pursue it. He then launched into a recitation of the materials I would need to amass in order to continue. It was a daunting list that included among other things all medical records from all the physicians I had seen over the past 10 years. The lawyer asked if I wanted to proceed. I had come to the moment of decision.

I demurred. I recognized the question and how I answered it for what it was – a major life turning point. My hesitation to proceed came not because I was reluctant to assemble the materials but because I was still reluctant to embark on a journey of retribution. It was not hard to imagine years of litigation that would monopolize my time and energy, leaving no time for actual living. I knew it would just concretize my bitterness, and I could never make peace with what happened and put it behind me if I went ahead. It was self-destructive. I would never get well; maybe physically I would, but never mentally whole if I continued.

Most importantly, I wanted to talk to the doctor again before I did anything. I wanted to believe in him. My gut sense and personal experiences told me he probably wanted, even needed, to confront the great unspoken thing between us—

mistakes had been made, and I suffered as a result—as much as I did. I also knew from personal experience that doctors have feet of clay. Even the best clinicians make mistakes from time to time. It was more important for me to understand how the mistake happened than to punish the physician for it.

Besides I knew from personal experience how easy it was to make a medical error of the most basic kind. Coumadin is a notoriously finicky drug with real dangers, life threatening ones, from over or under use. Preoccupation with proper dosing is common among Coumadin users as a result. In my case it bordered on an obsession because I had experienced excessive bleeding, clots and embolisms by deviating from the safe therapeutic zone. I always checked the dosage each day before I took the medicine. That is until one week when for some unknown reason, complacency, over confidence, inattentiveness, boredom, laziness – I don't know why, I let my guard down.

My normal daily dose of Coumadin was 8mg, a figure I achieved by taking two 2.5mg pills and a 3mg tablet. Coumadin tablets are color coded, 2.5mg pills are light blue and 6mg are darker blue with green flecks. One week, while loading the pill organizer, I must have grabbed the wrong bottle and substituted two 6mg pills for the two 2.5mg pills I normally took, effectively doubling the dose from 8mg to15mg. I took the pills for four days during which time I ingested more than a week's worth of Coumadin. The mistake was discovered serendipitously when a routine INR monitoring test came back abnormally high, 4.1. The INR would eventually top out at 6, two to three times the therapeutic range I was expected to stay within and nearly double the 3.3 reading I had when I once experienced an uncontrolled bleeding episode.

It is difficult to imagine how I could have made such a crude and dangerous mistake. I took only one medicine, once a day. It could not be a simpler task. I knew the risks of over or under dosing. I was in the habit of double checking the pills before taking them. No one could be more interested in making sure the treatment was followed to the letter. Yet despite all the simplicity and precautions I made a potentially serious and harmful mistake. It was a sobering lesson and an eye-opener of how easy it must be to err in more complex and ambiguous situations where time pressures and practice demands require real time judgments.

Professional Forgiveness

I learned firsthand at an early age about the effect medical errors can have on the caregiver. My father, a rural doctor from central casting for a Norman Rockwell painting, was as fallible as any other doctor and on occasion I was collateral damage from his mistakes. One incident in particular stays with me. A local farmer was struck by a rubber machine belt while performing an ordinary chore. At the time the belt was connected to a tractor's power takeoff in order to supply energy to run a piece of farm equipment that did not have a power source of its own, a common enough practice on a farm. For some reason the belt flew off the rapidly rotating power takeoff and hit the farmer in the temple. The man drove to town and was examined by my father, who subsequently sent him home. That night the man died of a cerebral hemorrhage.

Could his death have been prevented? Should my father have sent him to the nearby University of Michigan Medical Center for observation? Would they have been able to save his life? I have no way of knowing. What I do know is his only child, a son, was in my elementary school cohort, a group of not more than 60 pupils, and a fact that made me a lightning rod for his emotional distress.

The boy was absent for a while after his father's death. When he returned to school he was visibly angry and a great deal of his anger was directed at me. He avoided me. When contact was unavoidable he refused to look at me and we never spoke. Most disconcerting of all whenever I caught him looking at me his look could only be described as one of pure hatred. I was baffled. I had no idea what I had done to deserve his enmity.

Only when I mentioned it to my father did I learn the source of his hostility. My father described the accident, the office visit and that the man died the night after. The boy blamed him for his father's death he explained and the son was directing his anger at me, the daily reminder of my father's mistake.

As I grew older, I came to a more nuanced interpretation. The boy was no doubt very angry with my father but his anger with me had a different origin, I felt. I still had a father and my father was responsible for his father's absence. I was a constant reminder that the man who made the mistake still had a son and his son still had a father. The injustice of it must have been intolerable. Whatever the explanation the bitterness lingered. Ten years later as we prepared to graduate from high school never to see each other again the emotional stalemate remained. He never softened, I in turn never pressed the issue. We were bound together by a tragic twist of fate that could never be undone.

For his part my father was deeply affected by the man's death and his part in it. He may not have been responsible and there may not have been anything that could have changed the outcome but my father was not one to forgive himself easily. Each instance when he could have done better, at least by his self-assessment, weighed on him. One case in particular stayed with him throughout his life and was very much on is mind as his own death approached.

As he told the story to me in a letter, a letter I read as part of my eulogy at his memorial service, a local farmer came to his office one day and asked to see the "doc." He was ushered into the examining room but during a brief chat he presented no specific physical ailments. Instead, he seemed downcast, did not sit erect, make eye contact or speak with any enthusiasm or force. As a General Practitioner, my father treated the man's entire family and had for years. He knew there was a family history of depression and that the man's father had committed suicide. Despite all the clinical evidence of depression exhibited by the patient and presaged by his family history my father did not address his obvious clinical depression. He never forgave himself for what would ultimately prove to be a tragic and fatal omission.

In those days in Michigan all doctors were deputy corners and physicians frequently received impromptu calls to come to a fatality site to officially declare a person dead and determine the cause of death. One such call came in to my father a few days after the fateful office visit. He recognized the address and drove to the farm. There in the barn he found the man he had seen several days before hanging from a rafter. Not just any rafter, but exactly the one from which the man's father had hung himself some years before. If there is such a thing as divinely inspired justice, one could hardly imagine a punishment more keenly poetic.

As the years past, the tragic omission to offer appropriate and timely care weighed more heavily on my father. He took a six-month sabbatical from practice to take a fellowship in Psychiatry at the University of California at San Francisco. He joined and eventually became President of the Academy of Psychosomatic Medicine. And lastly, he became a pioneer in the Family Practice movement, helping to define the psychiatric content and standards that are now part of the specialty and Board qualifying exam. He was a charter fellow of the specialty and left private practice for a joint appointment in the Family Practice and Psychiatry Departments at the Medical University of South Carolina where he taught until his retirement.

While my father's reaction to his error may have been exceptional, perhaps excessive, I do not believe the emotions that led him to his actions are uncommon. Physicians are moral actors, they know when they are wrong. The vast majority are empathetic professionals, who know the stakes that ride on their actions, who tend toward perfectionism and abhor error. How they react to the realization they have erred is what differentiates. There is no doubt a spectrum of adjustment that accompanies the dissonance that stems from the gap between a doctor's self-esteem and beliefs about their skills and substandard performance on a particular occasion that ranges from arrogance and denial on one extreme to the self-flagellation and reaction formation my father exhibited on the other.

How then does a physician reconcile a failure to perform at an optimal level? There is an interesting parallel from delinquency research, (not suggesting that physicians who make mistakes are criminal or deviant in any way) which is relevant I think. Two theorists, Sykes and Matza, suggested that delinquents were not ignorant of or immune to social standards and that as a consequence they felt pressure to conform and abide by rules. In practice, delinquents are well aware when they violate social mores and experience remorse and guilt as a result. They are motivated to minimize the guilt feelings by adopting explanations of their behavior that absolve themselves from the responsibility of having committed the deviant actions.

Sykes and Matza called the explanations Techniques of Neutralization, although some might call them social rationalizations or defense mechanisms. According to the theorists Techniques of Neutralization come on five flavors:

1. Denial of Responsibility—the delinquent is the victim, trapped in a situation they cannot control,
2. Denial of Injury—the actions did not cause harm to the victim,
3. Denial of the Victim—the victim had it coming to them,
4. Condemnation of the Condemners—the victim is acting out of spite to accuse them of wrong doing,
5. Appeal to Higher Loyalties—in the long-term greater good will come from the delinquent act.

Techniques of Neutralization is a robust framework, and in my opinion, one that can be applied to large class of social situations where intentional actions, mistakes or even fate create victims. Physician error is one such category.

While I have not studied this issue rigorously, I imagine that some social rationalization is part of every physician's adjustment after having made a medical mistake. Rephrasing Sykes and Matza we might expect the general explanations for what happened to follow similar lines:

1. Denial of Responsibility—I wasn't the right person to handle the patient, but I had to act,
2. Denial of Injury—there was no lasting damage and the consequences could have been far worse—fitting for my case,
3. Denial of the Victim—the patient's lifestyle was the reason treatment failed,
4. Condemnation of the Condemners—it's the fault of the greedy malpractice attorneys,
5. Appeal to Higher Loyalties—physicians learn from their mistakes, as does the profession leading to better medical care in the long run – appropriate in my father's case.

Perhaps there are others. The important point is, however, Techniques of Neutralization are a socially and professionally functional ways to justify an error; they are an appropriate way to respond to an assault on a practitioner's competence and self-confidence. With guilt assuaged the physician is able to regain the poise and confidence required to continue to practice effectively. Techniques of Neutralization are a vocabulary of stock explanations, excuses if one takes the pejorative view, but nonetheless ready reasons that provide an avenue to move on, and a way for physicians to forgive themselves.

Personal Forgiveness

I wonder though if physicians ever afford themselves the luxury of unburdening themselves. If physicians are predominantly caring individuals who know when they are wrong, they must have some guilt about the suffering their lapses in judgment have caused another person. Unless, that is, they have learned to repress the feelings through distancing and objectivity. That guilt must be resolved in some fashion if they are to continue to practice effectively. So in a sense the recovery journey is a road travelled by two people, physician and patient in tandem.

If my physician were going through his own process of introspection regarding the care he provided before my PE or the role he played in my current situation, I would never know. He studiously avoided any mention of the pre-event care, let alone provided an explanation of how we got to that place. An apology if he felt I deserved one was beyond the realm of possibility. Instead, our contacts remained in the safe zone of clinical indicators and therapies, Coumadin dosages, diet, return to exercise, and lab values. What happened before was an insurmountable barrier between us.

There was the single break in the professional objectivity I mentioned previously. Somewhat out of the blue during a follow-up visit my physician asked me if I was depressed. It was a flash of insight on his part that I sincerely welcomed. I readily agreed that I was, expecting a discussion to follow. I was desperate to talk with him about my mental state and the reasons for my depression. More than anything else I wanted to ask him the questions I had asked other physicians. I wanted nothing more than to know why he had not taken steps that could have prevented my near fatal attack and its debilitating aftermath. I wanted to hear him acknowledge it was his fault, that he had been wrong and that he was sorry he had failed me.

The question represented additionally, the only time when I felt I was being regarded as a full human not just a lung or a leg. It filled a gaping psychic wound. I wanted someone to recognize, acknowledge and appreciate how difficult this experience was for me, to help me get through it. For better or worse, my physician and I were partners in my recovery. Like every marriage it was sometimes fractious, it took tolerance, empathy and adjustment to make it work. I wanted my physician say he was committed to helping me with this aspect of my return to health.

One step in this process was to deal with what happened in the months leading up to the PE, to recognize the mistakes and move on. But that would never happen. Without an opportunity to clear the air with my doctor, I turned to other resources. I sought out a friend and therapist with whom I could work through the tangled knot of post crisis emotions that my interactions with the physician only seemed to tighten.

For me, the therapy sessions were instrumental in regaining my psychological bearings. By this time I had fully repudiated the need to blame and shame my caregivers. Dwelling on the what-might-have-beens did nothing to alleviate my suffering, just the opposite in fact. It reinforced my feelings of having been the hapless victim, the unwilling and unwitting innocent patsy of a cruel injustice not of my making or the butt of some colossal cosmic joke played by a malevolent prankster. Perseverating on holding the bag for someone else's mistake did nothing but fuel my resentment, reinforce my feelings of helplessness and cause depression that brought my life to a complete halt. I had to move forward or become an emotional zombie, the living dead frozen in acrimony until actual death liberated me.

It was hard to move forward though. I was innocent, god damn it. But how innocent was I really? As the temporal distance from the emergency lengthened the intensity of the fear of a repeat attack and sudden death steadily waned, I turned the anger I had toward others inward. I began to examine how my actions in the months leading up to the attack contributed to the PE. The more I evaluated, the more I blamed myself for what happened. I knew in advance that I was very sick. I knew what the reason was—I was reminded each time I took a step or bent my knee to sit. Why didn't I demand to have an ultrasound? Barring that why didn't I seek a second opinion? Ultimately the responsibility for my health was not solely the doctor's, it was mine as well I concluded.

Beyond that the years leading up to my accident were especially trying for me, they were a stress-filled mess of my own making. I got involved in a start-up business that did not fare well with a partner I did not know well enough because of my lack of due diligence. The investment soured. Seeing the handwriting on the wall my partner the operational arm of the partnership, absconded leaving me, the supposed silent partner, to operate the business. It was a nightmare.

Physically the stress took a major toll. I was trapped in a situation that I never conceived, attempting to run a business I had little experience in, incurring losses that were previously unimaginable. Worse, the daily commute to the business was an hour each way. While there, I spent long hours standing and walking on a concrete floor. The commute and operational demands of the business aggravated and possibly even caused the DVTs that eventually spawned the PE.

The timing was confirmatory. I had an ultrasound of the offending leg just before investing in the business. It was unremarkable. The PE occurred three months after the business failed. These were precipitating circumstances that had nothing to do with my physician or the medical care he provided. In my most honest moments I knew I had to take responsibility for my share of what happened. In the last analysis, I was not such an innocent victim after all.

This period of self-evaluation and recrimination was the nadir of my journey back to emotional health. Anger, self-loathing and depression characterized my mental state. Still before I could understand the physician I had to understand myself, I realized. Before I could forgive him, I had to forgive myself. Both of our mistakes were contributing factors to my illness. Reconciling them and what they produced, forgiving the agent who caused the mistake were necessary ingredients in a complete recovery.

The Power of Apology

I recalled a client interaction from the early days of my consulting career that made an important impression on me and has stayed with me ever since. The name of my company was Consulting Statisticians, Inc. (CSI) something of a misnomer since the three of us who founded it had backgrounds in psychology, sociology (me) and subatomic particle physics. Not a statistician in sight. What we did share was strong quantitative orientation and an inability to succeed in institutional settings. Consulting Statisticians seemed to capture the essence of the partnership.

In the early days CSI did a wide array of projects many quite esoteric: just to name a few: statistical machine progress control for Scott Paper, election forecasting for ABC News, sales forecast models for Time Magazine, Monte Carlo simulations for emissions modeling for VW, the effect of advertising on long distance calls for New England Telephone and clinical trials analysis for a host of pharmaceutical companies, including Boehringer-Ingleheim for the bronchodilator drugs I would encounter again 35 years later. It was a dog's breakfast to be sure.

Among the disciplines on staff were two engineers who specialize in human factors (ergonomic) product design. Redesign of something as basic as a toothbrush was one of their credits. The Reach toothbrush was the result. This, at that time, relatively rare specialty brought Fisher-Price to our door. Back in the day Fisher-Price was one of the most respected companies in the U.S and remains so today. It was a well-earned reputation. Their products were high quality, nearly indestructible, safe and educational. One of the pleasures of consulting was having the opportunity to work with and learn from companies like Fisher-Price.

The brief described by the client was an odd one, far out of character given their corporate reputation. After a few minutes of discussion it was clear the problem had shaken the company to the core. Six families whose children had been killed while playing with a relatively benign toy had sued Fisher-Price. The corporate lawyers who visited us were less concerned about finding evidence to exonerate the company than finding a way to redesign the product to prevent future tragedies.

The product in question was a weapon of some sort; I don't really recall what kind. Any kind of weapon was a departure for Fisher-Price. The toy shot a projectile, a very soft one at a very slow rate of speed. For some reason children seemed to like to put the toy in their mouths and shoot the projectile, an action that proved fatal to six children. Fisher-Price wanted to determine if there was some attribute that enticed children to play with the toy in this manner and to redesign it if possible.

In the course of the conversation, one of the attorneys related a story of a trip the product manager responsible for the toy took to meet one of the grieving families. Ostensibly the trip was to investigate the facts of the fatality, but in the process the obviously shaken manager expressed how devastated he was about what happened. It was a cathartic moment for both the manager and the parents. When it was over the parents told the manager they had decided to drop the suit. A financial settlement was never their aim they said, they just wanted to know someone cared about what happened to their child.

For me the story has always been a parable of the healing power of apology and the reciprocal healing power of forgiveness. The memory of it affected me deeply while I recuperated after the PE because it offered so many parallels with my own circumstance. I never wanted to use malpractice as a cudgel to punish the physician for his errors real or imagined. It was never either my ticket to the medical malpractice lottery, a way to profit from bad fortune at his expense. I only contemplated action when I thought I was being ignored and unappreciated.

The fallacy of medicine as it is practiced in contemporary America, I think, is we expect physicians to be infallible. We have no tolerance for human imperfection. We cannot accept the awful truth that even the best doctors make mistakes and people will be hurt because of them. But physicians operate on a continuum of grace as we all do, some days they are better practitioners than on others. It is tragic that patients can be damaged, harmed and debilitated in the process but I am convinced only in the rarest of cases of gross negligence or incompetence does this rise to the level of malpractice.

In business successful managers aim to be right more often than they are wrong. Physicians are held to a more exacting standard where no error is without consequences, second-guessing and the specter of legal action. In the era of social media it can only get worse. A physician's reputation can be tarnished with a one-way unanswerable accusation. It is an easy and anonymous way to get retribution and revenge, to blame and shame on line where the accused has no opportunity to respond.

It is the fate of some of us to be the recipients of the effect from the cause, to be the person who suffers and is diminished by the error. I put great stake in the role of probability and chance in every day affairs. Occasionally our luck is just plain bad, results fall below our expectations, and far below our wishes. Sometimes sutures happen. At one time or another they may happen to each of us as chance dictates. Excluding rare cases of gross negligence and a pattern of incompetence there is in my mind no room for blame, no reason for retribution.

The second law of thermodynamics rules our lives. It foretells our aging and our demise. It is the arrow of time that dictates our lives only move one way. Mentally, it is always possible to reverse the one way arrow, to backtrack and to find a way to a better place. But it didn't happen and what did happen cannot be undone. We are all victims of myriad contingencies and aleatory risks. Eventually they can catch up and overtake us.

Although we cannot change the past the future is not determined, we do have a hand in creating the journey's route even if it is one way. Accepting that we can be the victims of bad luck, which may include bad judgment, is not fatalism, it is realism. We are no more victims than we are if we lose in the genetic lottery. So although the physician's mistakes may have been the proximate cause of my medical crisis it was part of a chain of causation and near the end of it as well. Even though I would never get an apology or have the opportunity to discuss what happened with my doctor I could accept and forgive his contribution to the terminus of the chain as I could my own for setting it in motion.

The real tragedy for medical practice in our litigious contemporary society is there is no safe place in which physicians can apologize if so inclined without exposing themselves to reputational and financial damage. Forgetting for a moment the obvious financial burden the revenge machine creates, over testing, over prescribing, malpractice insurance costs and so forth, the psychic impact to physicians and patients alike of this medical omerta is enormous I believe. In the aftermath of major medical crisis, a place to resolve without recrimination, apologize if need be and forgive is a necessary component of the healing process. At least it was for me.

Epilogue

Regarding my malpractice quandary, my forbearance was rewarded ultimately. For days despite specifically requesting a call back from the physician I had not received one. There was no indication on my cell phone either of received but unanswered calls or messages waiting. The effrontery of it was incongruous to me. It did not square with the person I thought I knew. I wanted to talk to the doctor, to discuss therapies of course, but also to clear the air. But now it appeared I was without that option.

I was resigned to moving ahead with legal remedies. All the same, I decided first to check my phone messages just to be sure. To my very great surprise and relief, I found seven personal calls from the physician over the preceding three days. Each one was delivered in a patient and calm tone, betraying no trace of anger, frustration or irritation. I was gratified by his persistence, by the fact that he did not just leave the matter with one obligatory call back, but made a concerted effort to make contact. I am not ashamed to admit it was a form of the ego stroking I sought.

I was instantly unburdened. All the resentment and anger I carried, like some enormous block of ice that froze my outlook on life, simply melted away. The messages reaffirmed my faith in the person and the practitioner. It was not the apology and cathartic conversation I envisioned or once hoped for, the time for that was gone, but the functional and symbolic significance was the same. Going forward I knew I was in a partnership, part of a team that would work to bring me back to good health. Since then, our relationship has grown and matured, become solid and dependable, nurtured and solidified by a deepening foundation of trust on both of our parts. What started as a marriage of convenience is now a union of common purpose. Going forward we are partners in this endeavor for better or worse, in sickness and in health.

CHAPTER FIVE
FACING OBLIVION

"Nothing is more dreadful in life than the profound thought that death may only greet you with eternal nothingness."

—*Kim Elizabeth*

(1954 –)

There is a faith gene. I know this for a fact because I don't have one. I am convinced it is waiting to be found by the Human Genome Project. Then perhaps I can get in line for genetic reengineering to fill the void left by my lack of faith. But I got the empirical gene instead. If god is not confirmable by one of the five senses I cannot accept it. Faith is no substitute for scientific proof for me unfortunately.

I wish I did believe in god. It would make the swirling, looming thoughts and emotions set in motion by a medical emergency so much simpler, less frightening, and more endurable. It is not as if I have not tried to believe, to have a personal relationship with god or to know and accept the spiritual underpinnings of life. To the contrary, much of my intellectual life has, in fact, been a struggle to come to terms with the end of life and the profound mystery of our existence, what, if anything, comes after. But I always come back to the same place, show me proof.

My parents did not shirk from their religious instructional responsibilities either. Church attendance weekly, catechism training and confirmation were all part of my preteen years.

My father in particular led by example. Reading scripture to us at the breakfast table and kneeling with us to pray at bedtime. But I remained spiritually challenged. Like an actor without empathy for the character he portrays, I could recite the lines but mouthed them in a dead pan voice of nonengagement.

Having been raised in a Protestant denomination I understood death to be a grand reckoning. Life's commencement exercise where the good students graduated to a higher level while the ones who did not learn their lessons were held back to do remedial work in a more structured, considerably stricter environment for all eternity. Perpetual summer school for the damned if you will.

I understood these beliefs best in commercial terms. Life was a going concern summarized by a balance sheet where good deeds, pure thoughts and piety were on the asset side while personal failings, unkindness, doubt and especially nonbelief were liabilities. Death marks the points when the Grand Accountant will read the entries and determine if my life had equity and deserved a paradisiacal promotion. Or if not and the liabilities exceeded the assets, my life had no net worth and I would be turned over to the Grand Receiver for eternal liquidation.

But being on the point of death does have a way of profoundly challenging a person's conceptions of life and death. Especially when it happens abruptly and without warning so there is no opportunity to put up well-rehearsed defenses against death, to keep them from entering our thoughts and disrupting our prosaic lives. Instead there is just the empty abyss of death, the mortality we know we all share and will be our end. There is nothing between this realization and knowing the caprice of life, the final fallacy of continued existence. Beliefs and conceptions of life after death, whether devout, agnostic or atheistic, which permit a modicum of stability in our lives, are not there to protect us.

First of all there is the question of dying. What will it be like? Will it be quick and painless or will I suffer? How will I behave at that moment? Will I be stoic, resigned to fate, or rapturous to meet God and receive an everlasting reward for a life well lived or simply so frightened all decorum will be lost? Personally, I always suspected I would be in the latter category. Without faith to fall back on there was no reason not to believe that death would mark the point of nonexistence for all time. I can think of no more terrifying thought. The big 3-D TV screen goes off. There is no test pattern, no national anthem; just nothingness for all time. I only hoped that at that moment I would not embarrass myself by making a scene.

Fortunately perhaps, I've had practice runs over the past few years. At times, in fact, I felt like I was the leading character in the Final Destination film franchise. Even before the PE on the beach and the complications after, I narrowly escaped death by drowning on a dive trip to Bali. It was one of those instances where you seem to be buddied up with a guy named Murphy. If there was something else that could have gone wrong on the dive, I can't imagine what it could have been.

It was a spur of the moment dive, the objective of which was to see a Mola Mola, an odd shaped flat, squarish creature with ridiculously tiny fins on the top and bottom of its body, no tail to speak of, that tips the scales at a ton or more when fully grown. Mola Mola are uncommon. Despite hundreds of dives I had never seen one. It was too good an opportunity to pass up. We rode to the dive site through 6 to 8 foot seas, not particularly threatening but nauseating just the same.

The dive was a last minute, some would say impetuous, decision. We were using rented equipment as a result. Although near the equator the water was freezing cold necessitating the use of a heavy wetsuit, which are constricting on the best of occasions and claustrophobic on this one. The other equipment such as a buoyancy compensator vest, instrumental in maintaining a constant depth, and regulator (air source) were equally unfamiliar and ill fitting. All the gauges were in metric units necessitating mental gymnastics to determine depth and amount of air remaining. That would have mattered if I could see the gauges, but I could not through the rented mask. While under water I had no idea of the depth but I was fairly certain it was more than 130 feet, the recreational dive limit, meaning the bends were a possibility upon ascent if precautions were not taken.

We swam underwater against a strong current to the point of an island where the Mola Mola were reported to be. Rounding the point we were met with a ripping crosscurrent so violent I could not maintain position or depth. I tried to swim against it without success. Eventually, I grabbed the coral encrusted rocky outcrop that formed the point of the island and hung on for dear life lest I be swept away. Suddenly a counter surge slammed me against the coral outcrop. My regulator was torn from my mouth and I began to inhale water. Tendrils of blood began to stain the water. I looked up at the surface. It was so very far away, I'd never make it.

I grasped futilely for the air hose flapping behind me in the raging current. Instinctively my training and experience kicked in. I dropped my weight belt and rose rapidly toward the surface impossibly far above, my last chance to survive. I vividly recall thinking as I ascended: So this is what it is like to die. This is where life ends and the great questions will be answered. Surprisingly, there was no dread, no panic, no desperate yet frantic attempts to change the outcome. A profound calm overcame me. Tension left me replaced by wonder and expectation.

My life did not flash before my eyes, I am sorry to say. I did not lose consciousness and need to be brought back. So I had no opportunity to experience, or not, the iconic near death visions and sensations others often report. I did however have enough time to give up hope and accept the inevitable. For someone who always feared making a scene and embarrassing themselves while dying, the moments of calm and curiosity were deeply reassuring. I will never again fear the moment of death.

But, of course, that episode and the insight it provided only speaks to the moment of death and not what happens, if anything, after. It is this question more than any other that a near death event forces to the surface of consciousness and keeps there. It demands an answer. In the extreme the experience can leave survivors fixated on finding an answer to the point it becomes a pathological preoccupation. Lives becoming nonlives because of the fear of permanently not living; fear so great it causes in some the equivalent of paralysis and catatonia. A life not lived for the fear of not living, the irony is bitter.

Unlike many who survive a brush with death I did not have a religious cushion to rest on. I had no eschatological architecture among my beliefs I could reference and enjoy the ready answers it provided. Like many faithless, I imagine, I began to search for answers to the great mystery in the end-of-days narratives of various religions, trying on different suits to see if any fit. It is not as if this was my first bout of spiritual and religious grazing. In one way or another I had been engaged in this pursuit of the meaning of life on and off throughout my life. The difference was now it took on an air of urgency.

Everywhere I turned it seemed the dialogue surrounding near death, real death and life after death drew on a rich foundation of religious language, images, expectations and beliefs. It was as if it were impossible to talk meaningfully without references to god – god's plan, intercession, beneficence. Equating survival to god-given good fortune – a miracle – is just one such example.

Miracles

Miracles do happen. At least that is the solemn affirmation that often accompanies survival against long odds. But do they?

Take as an example my pulmonary embolism. As best I can tell, and there are precious few statistics in the popular or medical literature to go on, my chances of surviving the first five minutes once the PE struck were, at best, one-in-three, and of surviving at all was maybe a fifty-fifty proposition. Case in point, I did survive. Does that constitute a miracle?

My wife certainly thought so. While trying to make sense of my good fortune she would quote her mother, a holocaust survivor – a woman who was no stranger to death, life and the capricious difference between the two. "We live with miracles" my wife said to me on more than one occasion before bursting into tears at the enormity of it all. She was, of course, speaking metaphorically – or was she? Did she believe a miracle had truly happened? If so, how could she differentiate it from something more prosaic like "being lucky" and beating the odds?

Let's think about this for a moment. What is the counterfactual for a death defying survival? The converse of the miraculous escape from death is: a person who did not "cheat" death; they died when in the same situation. No one marvels or talks about curses or divine intervention in that case. Death was the likeliest outcome and the odds were not beaten. So, do we need anything more than chance to explain why life or death is the outcome? Why is it necessary to use such a pregnant term as miracle in order to make sense of the competing causes and consequences, odds and chances, in other words fate?

We could just as easily invoke the rationality of the law of large numbers and accept that the likelihood of death will approximate the average mortality rate for the cause over the long haul. But this makes little sense in the individual case. For a person in the moment there are no fractions, no rates, chances, odds or mortality estimates. The calculus is much simpler, 1 or 0, yes or no, dead or not. When the time comes we are all individuals not biostatisticians. Then too the magnitude of the loss avoided, for ourselves and others if we are loved, contributes to the designation of the fact as miraculous or not. Not dying may qualify as a miracle, not losing an arm may not.

Miracles do seem to appear with some regularity, at least given how often the word is used, perhaps even too often to qualify as miracles. So how often do miracles actually occur in real life? It may be best to view this question mathematically. We know the number of events that occur in defiance of the odds, the ones we deem to be miracles. We observe these. But what about the ones we observe and count that play out exactly as we expect? In epidemiological speak, what is the incidence and case mortality of PE's? In other words how many cases of PE's occur in a time period and how many of these result in death? For that matter, what about all the occurrences that did not result in an observable outcome at all? In the case of PEs, all the small clots that did not cause enough impact to rise to the level of awareness let alone treatment. So we are left with one incomplete equation

$$\text{Miracles} = \text{PE's survived} / (\text{PE Incidence} + \text{PE Case Mortality} + \text{Unobserved PEs})$$

The proportion of events that are deemed to be miracles is unknown because all the terms in the denominator are not known accurately.

Even if it were possible to calculate the odds precisely we would have a definitional problem. What does the fraction in the preceding equation need to be in order to qualify as a miracle? Less than one in a million perhaps? The equivalent of winning the lottery? How about being struck by lightning, a good analogy, and one that has relatively precise meaning, since over the past three decades on average 53 people a year in the US are killed this way. In any given year the odds are 53 deaths among 320,000,000 people or .00000017 to 1. Mathematically that would seem to qualify.

Something more fundamental is going on clearly. Humans have an inherent and inherited need to explain what happens in their lives, a compelling motivation to make sense of the vast array of otherwise Brownian actions and consequences that surrounds us. Acting on this need conferred an evolutionary advantage to the species, allowing it to avoid destruction when we were few and weak and to mold the environment to our liking when we became strong and numerous. The ability to pair cause and effect with certainty is the hallmark of the species' dominance.

But chance is the antithesis of cause and effect, unless you are a statistician or physicist with a high tolerance for probabilistic outcomes, that is. For most of us chance, luck, fate, is the definitional opposite of certainty. It is evidence that god does play dice with the universe and humans are the die that die.

The human psyche has a hardwired need to understand – to identify cause and consequence – to find an explanation, a reason for events no matter how rare an occurrence. Viewed in this light, miracles are the shorthand to explain why something happened when all other explanations are insufficient or when events propelled by mindless and impartial chance are too frightening to contemplate. In the last analysis miracles are a portal into a well of spirituality that redeems misfortune by seeing it as part of an omniscient design and realization of a divine preference that provides purpose.

Miracles, of course, have a spiritual connotation – an undercurrent of divine intercession. An outcome should have occurred but it did not. The victim should be dead but they are not. No amount of ratiocination of the sort "if the clot had been a centimeter bigger you would have died" can dissuade the feeling that something truly extraordinary happened and if one is inclined to religious interpretations of life events, it had divine origins. A feeling persists of having been spared the otherwise inevitable by a benign power personally intervening on one's behalf to tip the scales, to rig the balance of fate, in our favor. It is a short step from miraculous survival to presumed divine revelation and the belief, by oneself and others, that one is chosen. They were spared by a higher power in order to do great things. The miraculously saved are called to a greater purpose.

But as I said I lack the faith gene. It seems to an agnostic like me that miracles are nothing more than a name and meaning believers give to rare events for which they have no acceptable rational explanation. The meaning surviving a near death encounter conveys to the agnostic, by comparison, is not associated with the cause but rather the consequence. The cause is chance and no divine intervention is required to explain it. But the consequence can be as fraught with significance for the agnostic as the believer. While I would never intimate I was the beneficiary of god's intercession or a chosen instrument god's will thereafter I share with my believer counterpart the feeling that my life has been transformed in profound ways. We each have a keen awareness of the capricious and fleeting nature of existence. We share a compelling need to imbue our lives with meaning through purposeful action to maximize the productive use, however we may define it, of what remains. Perhaps this is the true miracle of having survived.

The Power of Prayer

Prayer is in some respects an extension of the miracle hypothesis but with a twist. It is the difference between beating the odds and rigging the game.

Shortly after my second PE while I was recovering in the hospital I received an email from my sister meant to offer sympathy and support; she wrote:

> *Joe, I believe strongly in the power of prayer, and I am praying that the Lord will strengthen your spirit and give you inner peace so that you will be able to face all the challenges that life presents. We, us siblings, have already been blessed with strong family and friend connections that bring us comfort and strength in hard times as well as good; but the most important thing, again I believe, is to lean on a power that is infinitely greater than all of us combined.*

Obviously, my sister got the faith gene. I'm not sure what this implies about the heritability of my lack of faith. Maybe it is a recessive trait or atheism is a mutation.

This email is typical of the supportive communications and interactions one is apt to receive during convalescence from some dire disease or in anticipation of an equally dire procedure. These may not be as simply put or as eloquently stated, as the one I received from my sister but essentially the message is the same, there is a higher power that looks after us and gives us what we lack and need in times of tribulation. The succor provided may be as benign and unobtrusive as described in the prayer offered by my sister, that "the Lord will strengthen your spirit and give you inner peace," in order that I might "be able to face the challenges that life presents." Or for those who profess to have taken Jesus as a personal savior, it may be egocentrically utilitarian, where prayer beseeches god for the granting of a specific desired resolution to the problem of the day no matter how trivial.

For Christians the promise for this omnipotent beneficence, as we know from the under-eye shade of countless athletes and placard carrying fans who routinely position themselves directly under the basket while an opponent attempts free throws, is given in John 3:16

> *For God so loved the world, that he gave his only*
> *begotten Son, that whosoever believeth in him*
> *shall not perish, but have everlasting life.*
> (King James Version)

It is a simple quid pro quo, personal belief in and devotion to god in exchange for assistance in times of need and salvation at the end of life. Think of it as a cosmic charity for the chosen.

Cynicism aside, the belief that devout invocation in times of need will be met with divine intervention in specific individual's lives transports belief in god from the realm of faith into the domain of existence. The power of prayer is the bridge from supernatural causality, accepted without evidence, to testable propositions and proof from observable phenomena. If god exists, prayer should work in other words. Does it?

This question has been taken up recently by several research teams in teaching hospitals, domestic and foreign, that have looked at the effect of intercessory prayer, where one person prays for another as my sister did for me, on recovery times and overall medical outcomes, the most important being mortality. The studies use proven research methods to eliminate all possible explanations other than prayer as the cause of any observed difference between prayer and no prayer groups. In the most rigorous studies, subjects are assigned to a treatment group, prayer or no prayer, at random so no attribute of the participant, like a faith gene, will bias or confound the findings. Any difference in the groups will be solely a matter of which received prayer as a consequence. The person praying for them is also randomly assigned so whether or not a person is prayed for and if so, by whom is simply a matter of chance.

Typical of these sorts of studies is one from the Mind/Body Institute at Harvard Medical School. In this instance 1,802 patients recovering from coronary artery disease bypass surgery were assigned in equal numbers to one of three groups: 1) a group receiving intercessory prayer after being told they might or might not be prayed for, 2) a group who were similarly informed that they might or might not receive prayer but did not, and 3) a prayer group who were told in advance they would be prayed for. Essentially then, there were two variables tested: intercessory prayer-yes or no, i.e., groups 1 vs. 2, and knowledge of receiving prayer-yes or no, i.e., groups 2 vs. 3.

Participants in the study received intercessory prayer for 14 days starting the day before surgery. The test outcomes followed were: any complications, major events or death within a 30-day window post-surgery. At the end of the period there were no important differences between the three groups on the incidence of major events or mortality. The results for any complication post-surgery were more intriguing. The two groups who were uncertain about whether they received intercessory prayer had comparable rates of complications, 52% for those who received prayer and 51% for those who did not. However, those certain of having been prayed for were 14% more likely to experience complications than those who were uncertain; 59% for the former and 52% for the latter, a finding that was unlikely to have occurred by chance.

One explanation for this counterintuitive and potentially detrimental effect suggested by the authors was those who knew they were being prayed for interpreted it as an indication of being in need of prayer. Perhaps as a result the knowledge-of-prayer group was more apt to believe they had complications and report them. Or more ominously, they might have been induced to have a deleterious psychosomatic reaction when informed strangers were praying for them, a reaction that actually affected their response to surgery or recovery from it.

The major take-away of the preceding study was intercessory prayer was not effective and conversely might be detrimental to a patient's recovery if they know people are praying for them. Needless to say the findings were controversial and sparked a back and forth debate in the literature. Other studies, additionally, have found positive effects for intercessory prayer. So the benefits of prayer for the sick seem to be equivocal depending on study. Nevertheless, the final word may reside with a review of 10 studies involving 7,646 patients in all, conducted by a team in England. The team could find no evidence for positive benefits accruing from intercessory prayer when the results of all the studies were combined.

So praying for others doesn't help and god remains inscrutable. Why then the preoccupation with prayer for the sick? My sister knows full well I am an atheist and she must also know that her entreaty will fall on deaf ears. So why would she persist? The obvious answer is given twice in the email, "I believe." The email is a profession of her faith not mine. The benefit must accrue to her not me as well. Is this a just matter of self-reinforcement of belief? Is it another asset to enter in the general ledger of life? Could it be obligatory, a social pretense, so just a way to avoid deeper involvement? Or was it projection, what she would want for herself under the same circumstances? Maybe on some level all of these reasons were operative.

At worst offering prayers can be a minimalist expression of assistance proffered more as a guilt assuaging mechanism for not doing more or at best an empty figure of speech. In either case it provides more psychic benefit for the giver than the receiver. An extreme example of this happened to me one day on the occasion of one of my many and varied athletic injuries. This time the implement of destruction was a bicycle.

I was in the habit of doing a twice weekly circumnavigation of my home Sanibel Island, from the lighthouse on the east end, through the wildlife refuge, to Blind Pass on the west end and back, a trip of about 30 miles. On the backside of the tour one day I was taking advantage of a straightaway to relax briefly by leaning out over the bike and resting my arms and upper body weight on the handlebars. Suddenly I hit a utility cap in the road. The bike lurched. In my precarious position I started to lose balance. The bike wobbled as I tried to right myself. I almost made it but at the last moment I squeezed the lever for the front brake. The wheel locked. The bike stopped. I did not. I went flying over the handlebars landing largely face first in the street.

I lay there in a daze for a few moments looking at the twisted bike frame a few feet away. Shimmering spots swam across my vision. I tried to yell to another biker in the distance but not much came out and unhearing he rode on. I could not stand but I was able to crawl to the side of the road dragging the ruined bike behind. I called 911 and sat waiting their arrival, as my white t-shirt was turned red by blood dripping from numerous facial lacerations.

A Good Samaritan drove by and stopped to give aid. I told him help was on the way and that I would be alright in the interim but he insisted on waiting with me until the EMTs came. As we waited together another car came by. It slowed. The rear window lowered and a face emerged from the dark interior. "We're praying for you" a woman called out. The car kept on without losing speed.

I have always wondered what possessed the observer to say such a ridiculous and impotent thing. No doubt it was a well-meaning expression of support. But from where I sat it was an empty gesture. Like the biblical Samaritan, my roadside companion, provided much more assistance and comfort than the pious passerby. My only regret about the incident is, although I asked him his name, I could not remember it the next day and I was never able to thank him properly. My guess is though that this bothers me now more than it does him.

Tent Revival

As a skeptic, the notion of the power of prayer and more generally faith reminds me of what I once observed while attending a tent revival. Some years ago an itinerant preacher and his band set up an enormous tent on the fringe of town and blanketed the area with a blitz of below-the-radar media consisting primarily of posters seemingly nailed to every telephone within a five mile radius. The posters promised a ministry of healing, not metaphorical healing, but faith healing of actual physical maladies. This was tantamount to miracles on demand, the power of prayer demonstrated in real time.

As a sociologist by training and practice I have always been intrigued by the boundaries of social action, the crucibles at the edge of societal conduct where meaning is made. Religious expressions from the far fringes of belief like tent revivals are laboratories filled with brewing eschatological meaning, like the places in the cosmos where dust coalesces to form stars and enormous quantities of heat and energy are given off. The genius of human invention of meaning was sure to be on display so I decided to take in a service.

At the appointed time I arrived and was ushered to my seat, a folding wooden chair placed temporarily on the grassy floor under the tent top. Soon a slick production started that followed a time-honored script, a ramp up of religious fervor followed by a show of healing culminating in an appeal for donations. Initially the crowd was warmed up by a hymn-singing choir of three beatific beauties dressed in angelic white gowns. They were followed by an understudy preacher who gave a rousing sermon in the upward lilting, songbird voice peculiar to evangelical ministers, consisting of one-line bites each punctuated by a drumbeat.

> "The Lord bless you"—Boom
> "And keep you"—Boom
> "And make his face to shine upon you"—Boom

After an hour of this spiritual carpet-bombing it was time for the main attraction. The Reverend appeared, dressed in black from head to toe, his equally jet-black hair was coiffed in a pompadour. He was a caricature, the spitting image of Johnny Cash.

The Reverend launched into a sermon of his own which consisted primarily of telling the audience how rich he was. Net worth $5 million is the figure I recall. I am not sure what the point of this self-serving soliloquy was other than to illustrate that the preacher was the recipient of god's providence and therefore by extrapolation that he had a god-given power to heal. Although it might just have been an advertisement of what was expected of the faithful after the show because about twenty minutes into his pitch, abruptly, almost mid-sentence, the preacher turned to the audience and asked in a jarring non sequitur, "Want to see some tricks?"

This was what the throng several hundred strong had come to see and they shouted their appreciation. A line of lame, infirm and shills no doubt formed waiting for a turn to go on stage and receive the preacher's healing touch. Once there, the preacher asked them to name their malady. He then closed his eyes, placed his hand on their forehead, and shouted a palliative prayer to the heavens. All at once his arm spasmed, his hand trust out giving the head on which it rested a sudden push as if the healing power of god were being transmitted down his arm into the waiting body of the afflicted like some high voltage spiritual electrocution. This caused the supplicant to fall backward into the waiting arms of two burly people-catchers who revived, righted and escorted the newly cured off stage to the awed gasps, shouts of amen and hallelujahs and the thunderous applause from the assembled faithful.

It was all pretty routine and increasingly tedious until the preacher took an interesting detour for one woman. She came to the stage complaining of chronic headaches and neck pain. The obligatory prayers were said, her head anointed with god's healing power as it was transmitted through the pious preacher's touch. She collapsed, was caught and brought back from ecstasy to her previous conscious state. This time though unlike the others she hesitated as if skeptical that a change had taken place. As she started to leave the stage, the preacher called out, "Wait. I know something about you that you do not know." The audience hushed as the preacher beckoned her back to him. "You have a tumor growing inside your belly," he shouted as he laid a hand on her midsection. "It's too small for the doctors to see but I felt it and **it is malignant!**" he cried. The healing choreography was repeated and the women left the stage presumably disease-free.

Watching the interaction I was struck by the pure and simple genius of it. The preacher had just cured the woman of a dreaded disease she did not previously know she had. The proof of the cure and by extension the preacher's divinely inspired healing power was the absence of a dangerous tumor, a tumor whose existence only he could detect because of the self-same god-given gift. Now anyone looking for a sign of the tumor, let's say a physician, would never find any since presumably the cure had eliminated it. The tautology of a divinely granted gift to heal had come full circle—absence of cause was proof of cure. It was proof perfect if one simply believed, had faith, that there was a tumor there to begin with, something that could not now be proven because it had been healed away. It was airtight, incontrovertible, the audacity was breathtaking.

That exhibition of religious performance art has always been for me an allegory of faith and the power of prayer. If you believe in god and the power of prayer to get his attention, then any positive or non-negative event after is evidence of his work. It is proof positive that god loves us and will take care of us. But what about when negative things, like death, happen you ask? Well we all knew were going to die sometime, right? So death is just the time god chooses to call us home. There is an answer for every contingency if you just believe. It's all a matter of having the requisite faith, a quality I sadly do not happen to have in abundance.

Death and Immortality

The act of dying may not be as bad as I once feared. I can imagine some parting whimsy – nostalgia for a life gone by to which I cannot return. A profound sense of loss of missing and being missed by loved ones no doubt. I expect few regrets to come at the end, for things I wish I had done differently but instead more general regrets that life could not go on for a while longer – all the disappointments and irritations aside, I do enjoy living.

What I learned in Bali though is the horror and dread I once thought would accompany dying, the grasping, pleading, and clutching to hold on to life a little longer is not likely to occur. The terror of what lies ahead I previously expected will be replaced instead by a sense of calm, wonder and expectation, if my past experience is any indication.

Any death no matter how horrible or lingering is endurable though if one is assured that something follows it. The greatest fear of all is that there will be simply nothing at all. That thought fills us with dread because we cannot imagine what it means. What is nonexistence? We have no way of learning what it is or what it means to not exist, without dying of course which would solve the problem but defeat the purpose.

I find little in ancient or contemporary thinking about death that adds insight or comfort. The language used to capture the essence of nonexistence is, for instance, profound only in its vacuousness. Here is an example: "where you are death is not, where death is you are not". Could anyone conjure a more empty and meaningless tautology? Unfortunately this kind of pronouncement masquerades as profundity in the death discourse. The fact is death, nonexistence, is unknown and unknowable and it scares the bejesus out of us for that reason.

The prospect of nothing after death creates angst too about the meaning and purpose of the life that we lead now. Without something waiting at the end of life there would seem to be no goal to focus our actions and hence no reason to behave in a particular way. How would it be possible to live with purpose knowing that it does not matter how we live? We cannot accept life as an end in itself unless it is moving us toward some afterlife goal it seems. More than that working toward salvation or some reward for a life well-lived provides a reason to behave in a particular manner in addition to giving our lives meaning and purpose.

The argument can be made that without the final judgment there is no incentive to act morally. The world would soon devolve into a Hobbesian morass of anomic individuals trying without constraint to maximize their circumstances at the expense of others. Belief in god and the practice of religion is a moral contract that keeps us in line. This apocalyptic vision does discredit, I believe, to the real and intrinsic benefits of acting morally, in concert with others and with treating them fairly. Essentially, the glue that holds society together is trust predicated on reciprocity. Do unto others as you would have them do unto you works apparently in the long run on a practical as well as religious level.

The Existentialists faced the prospect of existence and moral behavior in the absence of belief in god head on. In the shadows of World War II in the face of tyranny when so many stood by observers to abominations against their fellow man, a philosophy emerged where the purpose of existence was defined by the sum of the actions we do or do not make. For Existentialists life was simply that – existence until death and nothing more. From rejection of god and life after death and the concentration on living in the here and now, a philosophy of purposeful action evolved. Heroes act – they act despite not knowing if their actions will end well or poorly. Cowards stand idle, inert. The meaning and significance one's of life derives therefore from the willingness to take action, existence precedes essence as Sartre famously summarized.

Existentialism is a philosophy an agnostic can embrace. It implies a moral order without god or salvation, where behavior is all there is and how we choose to live defines our humanity. Life is an end in itself. We are not mendicants behaving properly in order to curry the favor and rewards of some omniscient and omnipotent god. But the real question we all want answered is not how to live in the face of inevitable nonexistence, but rather will we go on living or is nonexistence our fate. We know our conscious selves leave at the moment of death never to return. But does consciousness, the avatar we call a soul, live after the body perishes?

Theorizing about immorality is typically the province of religion and religious precepts dominate the ideas and discussion. Contemplations on immortality are only a religious exercise however because each of the world religions supply a ready-made intellectual architecture constructed to answer two fundamental questions of existence: 1) how did we get here – the creation story, and 2) what happens after we, our consciousness, dies – the Immortality Postulate. The rest is a code of conduct, the moral contract that will get a person from point A - birth to point B – life after death.

With respect to the Immortality Postulate there are two prominent competitive beliefs, resurrection and reincarnation. Christianity is a good example of the former and it can be a stand-in for other religions that propose salvation after death and eternal life in paradise for believers. After death Christians are resurrected, as Christ was, to live with god forever in heaven. Belief in the resurrection is the defining idea of Christianity therefore and a prerequisite for salvation. Resurrection is made possible only for believers in the one god who can make it happen. There is some controversy surrounding the rules for living and the existence of unpleasant alternatives to paradise, but the paradigm is generally consistent across Christian manifestations and religions in the Abrahamic tradition.

There is no credible scientific evidence to support this artifice. No studies, observational or experimental, to suggest that resurrection happens after death. Instead, science had its own creation and immortality stories, we just don't like the implications. Creation of the universe began about 14 billion years ago with a big bang and things have been on geological and Darwinian autopilot ever since. What about consciousness though? No less a scientific mind that Francis Crick spent an entire book arguing, persuasively in my opinion, that consciousness is the product of a network of billions of nerves working in concert. When the brains cells die, so does consciousness – irrevocably. As for immortality, science is definite on that point as well. Not only are humans not immortal but neither is the universe. At some point, trillions of trillions of years hence, the universe will cease to exist – die – when all the energy, its life force, finally leeches out.

Reincarnation is the Immortality Postulate of Hinduism, Buddhism, and lesser offshoots, and hence a grounding belief of roughly one-sixth of the world's population. The body dies, in this formulation, but the soul – the Self – lives on inhabiting a new corporal vessel after each death, exchanging one temporal body for another for all time. The essence of the person, the Self is eternal and immortal therefore. The origins of the belief in reincarnation are so ancient as to be lost in history. However, reincarnation is explained succinctly in the venerable Sanskrit poem of religious instruction, the Bhagavad Gita – The Song of the Blessed One.

The setting for the revelation of reincarnation is the prelude to a climactic battle between two warring royal families of antiquity in North India. Before the battle, a leader of one side and the eventual receiver of wisdom, Arjuna, drives his chariot between the two opposing armies and pauses to contemplate the slaughter he knows will soon ensue when his army attacks. Arjuna hesitates to join the battle, however, lamenting the inevitable destruction of so many of the enemy when he does, soldiers in the beauty of their full manhood, and their leaders many of whom are his relatives. As he tries to decide what to do, fight or not, his chariot driver, the disguised Krishna, speaks up and exhorts Arjuna to fight. Among one of the god's arguments for war is contained in the following passage:

> These bodies come to an end;
> but that vast embodied Self
> is ageless, fathomless, eternal.
> Therefore you must fight, Arjuna.
>
> If you think that the Self can kill
> or think it can be killed

you do not well understand
reality's subtle ways.

It never was born; coming
to be it will never not be.
Birthless, primordial, it does not
die when the body dies.

Knowing that it is eternal
unborn, beyond destruction
how can you ever kill?
And whom could you kill, Arjuna?

Just as you throw out clothes
and put on other clothes, new ones,
the Self discards its used bodies
and puts on new ones.

Assume for a moment Krishna isn't just a skilled extemporaneous rationalizer trying to get an existential coward to man up and act, what value is reincarnation belief to a person who has recently looked nonexistence in the face? To be perfectly frank, I can find little solace in the concept. I might think differently if we could recall our past lives, see them like the receding faces of our reflection in facing mirrors. But outside of the reports from hypnotic regression or though meditation, it would appear that Bridey Murphy and the Lama's sister self are not accessible to the rest of us.

Even if we could "prove" reincarnation was a fact would it help us in this life? All the evidence suggests not. We still must die, our current life must end and awareness of it will not be carried forward to the next life as awareness of our last life was not carried forward to this one. Whatever happened in our preceding incarnations does not help us in this life and hence we cannot expect this life to be remembered or influence the next. If immortality is the legacy of our preceding lives, we do not have one. So even though if we are reincarnated it certainly looks from my perspective that the life we have now, our self, very much ends with our death.

Buddhism has an interesting slant on reincarnation based on the notions of impermanence and suffering. For Buddhists all "compounded" things are impermanent, constantly in flux, continually changing. All things are destined to pass away. Attachment to impermanent things, possessions as an example, leads to dissatisfaction and suffering. It isn't the things themselves that cause dissatisfaction but rather the objectification of them and our desire for them. It is only when we accept the impermanence of all things that we can be freed of our desires for them and suffering will cease.

The self is one such objectified thing. We delude ourselves that the self, our being, is an entity in its own right and that it is somehow immutable for all time. Our desire to hold on to life, to possess it and not lose it causes suffering in the face of death and the cessation of life. Buddhists believe therefore that suffering is destined to follow us in future lives unless we deal with it in this one. The contemplation of death, meditation on it, in order to destroy the delusion of self so we can let go of our desire for life is the door to liberation from suffering and more importantly the impetus for us to act morally. In this regard Buddhism and Existentialism have much in common.

I am sure I do a disservice to the complexities of Buddhist thought with my gross simplifications and will earn the scorn of many Buddhists and scholars as a result. But my goal is not to teach Buddhism but rather to point out its relevance to the experience and recovery from facing oblivion caused by a near fatal experience and its value for those that have. What the medical crisis does more than anything else is radically shatter any delusion we harbor that we are or can be immortal. It brings death out of the repressed regions of our psyche into bold, unignorable relief.

The experience is one of being held by the nape of the neck and cantilevered over an abyss, only to be pulled back at the last moment before falling. With the glimpse into the gaping chasm of nonexistence the delusion of the self shatters. We are forced to confront the fallacy of our ability and desire to hold it forever. Whereas in our daily lives we can keep thoughts of death at bay after the crisis they are never fully caged or will be again. I for one can find nothing in religious teachings, thought or precepts that will put my Humpty Dumpty delusion of self back together again.

The near fatal event propels the survivors into the reexamination and introspection the Buddhists advocate: to know that life is finite, the self is a delusion and attachment to it causes our suffering, and contemplation of death frees us from the suffering by making death familiar and acceptable. It is hard to argue with this thought structure given it is the path most survivors of near death have been involuntarily propelled along. For me it is the one belief system that offers a path to freedom from being the prisoner of thoughts and fears of nonexistence.

Even so, should consciousness cease upon death what is the legacy we leave? This too is a form of immortality.

Personally, I subscribe to a form of limited immortality. We live as long as we are remembered and our memory continues to influence the lives of others. For a few, limited immortality is a reflection of their fame. For most of us, it extends only as long as those who had personal knowledge of us exist. We live after death in the residual effect our interaction with others and our life has reciprocally shaped the behavior and humanity of the other. The echo of our lives reverberates down a cavern of time moving ever deeper but getting weaker as it moves away from us. Beyond that we are pictures in an album, the embers from a fire lit by our memory that, like us, has died. The curious thing is that in this view some of the great religious leaders, Siddhartha, Christ, Mohammad and others, are indeed immortal for all practical purposes. But unfortunately so are some of the Great Satans of history.

Limited immortality is what I expect after I die. I did have one strange thought, however. Suppose after death we get exactly what we believe in. I believe that we cease to exist and nothing more, so that's exactly what happens to me. If you believe in heaven, that's where you are bound. Reincarnation? Expect to be reborn over and over again for all time. I admit I have trouble with this theory when it comes to suicide bombers enjoying the favors of scores of virgins forever. And naturally I have no clue by what mechanism the disposition of souls would be effected, maybe a wormhole portal to alternate universes. But then being fuzzy on the details never slowed down any other belief system – that's what faith is for.

NDE's

I would be remiss in this discussion of immortality and empiricism if I passed over near death experiences (NDE's) without comment. NDE's are after all one area where we can potentially confirm the afterlife from people who maintain they have been there if only briefly. To be honest I don't know what to make of NDE's. The evidence is suggestive, tantalizing to be sure, but the cause and significance of NDE's are far from clear.

After more than three decades of conducting behavioral research I developed a high regard for the veracity and accuracy of human reporters. I have no doubt that the stories of those who have had an NDE are genuine reports of authentic experiences. They may not be real in an "objective" sense, independently measurable, but they are without question real for the person who has had one. People who have had an NDE are in short telling the truth about what they believe they have seen.

I am not alone in this regard. No less a student of death and dying than Elisabeth Kübler-Ross was a staunch proponent of the validity of NDE's, claiming to have compiled records of tens of thousands of such cases over the course of her career. She was convinced that the reports she heard were descriptions of actual experiences and were an indication of an afterlife her subjects had glimpsed. Dr. Kübler-Ross's strong spiritual orientation may have influenced her interpretation of NDE's however.

I am also impressed by the commonality in experiences of unacquainted people who claim to have had an NDE, the consistent reports of out-of-body experiences, narrowed vision, bright light at the end of a tunnel, feelings of peace and well-being, meeting a nonthreatening visage or deceased family member, etc. These experiences are so consistent that researchers have developed a short questionnaire that purports to confirm that a person has had an NDE. The necessary physical conditions for an NDE to take place are also known and accepted, restricted blood flow to the brain that causes cerebral hypoxia or oxygen starvation and hypercarbia, the buildup of excessive levels of carbon dioxide.

As a social scientist I also believe that if an experience is true in its perception, i.e., if the one who had an NDE believes it is real, it is true in its consequences for them. This is especially true for NDE's in that many who have had such an experience have been profoundly changed by it. One might say the same of anyone, myself and others, who has had a near fatal event whether they lose consciousness or not. Yet while our lives are changed, often profoundly, by suddenly facing oblivion, there is clearly something qualitatively different about an NDE as classically described. Those of us who have faced oblivion did not died per se, even fleetingly as NDE people have. We have no experience that will help shed light on the existence of an afterlife. The singular experience sets the NDE-er apart, making them an authority, rightly or wrongly, on immortality matters.

If factual, the NDE person has experienced the transition that we will all make eventually. NDE-ers are convinced they have been to heaven; they know without a scintilla of doubt it exists. Afterward they are privy to the answer to the greatest mystery of existence and have returned from the NDE as an explorer and guide to the next world. Little wonder then that many feel compelled to proselytize by sharing their revelations with those of us not as fortunate. Yet NDE-ers seem to have an inordinate need to "prove" the validity of the experience, that indeed heaven exists. The popular literature is replete with anecdotal attempts to convince the reader that no other explanation fits the facts.

So that settles it. NDE's are real and they give us a brief look at what dying and life after death will be like. They confirm that after death, we will transition to another state of being, a new realm of bodiless consciousness and they assure us the transition to the new state will be easy, even comforting. Most importantly NDE's **prove** that there is an afterlife and we, our souls, live on, perhaps not eternally, but at the very least our spiritual essence does not end with our physical death.

As you might well imagine, there are a few scientific obstacles to acceptance of NDE's as revelatory. First, there is the inability to completely rule out all other plausible alternative explanations for what happened. The problem with the evidence is, of course, that it is after the fact and cannot be replicated. It is impossible to use the tricks of experimental design, such as random selection and test and control groups, to systematically eliminate competing possibilities. Rigid experimentation aside, there is an opportunity compare people who have an NDE with those that do not, on such relevant criteria as clinical indicators, personal and background characteristics, especially religiosity. This research is in its infancy and not very illuminating as yet I'm afraid.

Moreover, only a small fraction of those who meet the criteria necessary to have a NDE, transitory brain death, actually have an NDE as classically described. The closest analog we have for return from actual death are people who have gone into cardiac arrest and subsequently been resuscitated. Of these, a small minority, only between 10 – 20%, report experiencing an NDE. What about the vast majority who do not? Are we to conclude that the transition to the new realm is not universal? Does it only happen to a chosen few?

Or does some other physical attribute, such the length of time the brain has been deprived of oxygen, explain why some experience an NDE and others do not? Are NDE's, as is often suggested, merely descriptions of the process of dying, the visions from the neural storm of a dying mind as the human CPU shuts down, later recalled and interpreted in religious terms when it is rebooted? Are NDE's like PTSD, a function of the over or under stimulation of specific brain structures?

Consciousness is not irrevocably ended in this case. So actual death and nonexistence have not yet truly been experienced. The NDE is nothing more than a description of the end of life in the moments immediately preceding death if this is correct. NDE's provides no evidence therefore, for or against, the reality of an afterlife.

The evidence on these competing views of NDE's is scant and ambiguous. One study found no relationship between religiosity and having an NDE. Another cross-cultural study found that while people share the objective aspects of NDE's, out-of-body experiences, bright lights, tunnels, and so forth, the interpretation of them by western European observers differs from those in other region. This in turn strongly suggests culture plays a large role in what is perceived and how the reporter describes and explains it.

And therein lies the fundamental problem with the reports of those who have had an NDE; they are inherently subjective and influenced by place and time. People who have an NDE describe the event and explain it by drawing from a reservoir of language, beliefs and shared cultural references with which they and we are familiar. This should not be surprising; the description and interpretation of all events are cultural constructions, understood by all people in relation to their social milieu.

Clinical Psychologists, as an example, might, consistent with their training, label the out-of-body experience often reported by those who have had an NDE as a dissociative reaction in response to a threat. Individuals who have strong religious training, ties and involvement, by comparison, might explain the NDE using readily available religious language and metaphors, hence as a brief sojourn in the afterlife. There is no real way to determine which is correct until we ourselves die.

Without doubt NDE's have hit a responsive chord among the reading public, indicating an unquenchable popular interest in life after death and the ability of NDE's to provide a peek at the other side. But I wonder. Has anyone ever had a negative NDE, a vision of hell they were destined for or is it all upside? One would think that if the Christian conception of life after death were accurate, there should be some NDEs that involve visions of eternal damnation manifest. Perhaps it is as simple as no one wants to write or talk about them.

The significance of NDE's to questions of immortality remains for now a fascinating mystery, therefore, and like beauty very much in the eye of the beholder. So where does this leave me, an inveterate empiricist, an agnostic with no faith gene? In the end, I remain a skeptical, even jaundiced, observer. Nonetheless one who has a desire to believe – agnostics always want to be convinced and atheists to be proven wrong – but unwilling and unable to accept anything on faith. I am waiting as ever for more evidence.

An Agnostic Doubts

Living without a faith gene can be rugged. Dealing with the loneliness that comes from not recognizing the omnipotent architect's grand design that others do is not fun. Resigned to the reality that you just don't "get it" and will never realize the joy and peace true belief can bring. Then just when I became comfortable with the psychic discomfort there comes along an event so weirdly coincidental that I doubt all my doubts.

About a month after the pulmonary embolism that nearly felled me there, I was back walking the same beach in an attempt to rebuild my stamina. It was late afternoon, the sky was slate gray and the beach was uncommonly empty. Just a single other stroller approached from the opposite direction. Our paths would cross at the site of my medical emergency. As we closed, my alter ego abruptly veered toward me and said without preamble, "May I ask you a question?" Our eyes met as I nodded assent, "Do you believe in god?" he asked. That took me back for a moment. Then I simply replied "No", lowered my eyes and kept walking.

I thought nothing of the incident at the time. But weeks later an odd thought crossed my mind. Suppose this was a refutation of everything I did not believe. What if this were the empirical evidence I had been searching for all my life? Could it possibly be that a divine presence had made itself know to me personally? Was I too preoccupied, too self-involved to notice?

What if, the Oceanside Inquisitor was a messenger from god I did not recognize? Could he be my "guardian angel" as a friend of mine maintained, come to ask "Did I make my existence known clearly enough yet? Or should the next attempt at persuasion be more convincingly severe?" Was this at last the empirical proof I sought before accepting the reality of god? Was it a miracle? Had my prayers been answered?

Unfortunately my genetic deficiencies left me unconvinced, without faith, existentially alone wanting for more evidence. Not able to bring myself to believe but hedging my bet by remaining open to the possibility, willing to walk around Mt. Kailash twice just in case.

CHAPTER SIX
WINNOWING—SHEDDING
AND LEAVING BEHIND

"One of the hardest lessons in life is figuring out
which bridges to cross and which to burn."

—David Russell

(1941 –)

When a person has a near death event, whatever the cause, they have coincidentally a sudden life event. A sudden life event is a symbolic watershed that irrevocably separates the past from the future, old from the new. It triggers a metamorphosing process of self-examination when the life one is living is reinterpreted in the focused reality of the lessons learned from the stark confrontation with sudden death. Rebirth may be too strong a term for it. Instead, it is more accurately an awaking to possibilities, often paired with an acute striving for meaning in life. It is a period of adjustment and testing when old patterns are evaluated and new ones are tried, when the future life course is reimagined.

For me it was as if the hard crust that surrounded me that was my past life was burst apart by the sudden life event. The super nova of my ego propelled me on an odyssey of self-discovery during which I tried to discover what really mattered to me, what I wanted to have and to hold, while letting go of the incidental and extraneous. The journey started tentatively at first gaining momentum and gravitas as time went on and my physical maladies diminished. It was a transformative experience of regaining equilibrium in the social world as I attempted to find a way to live the remainder of my life with peace and purpose.

Adjusting to sudden life events bears considerable similarity, with notable differences, to the process of preparing to die experienced by terminally ill patients as illuminated and codified in the seminal work *On Death and Dying* by Dr. Elisabeth Kübler-Ross. In Kübler-Ross's formulation of adaptation to the grief associated with the end of life, a person comes to terms with the certainty that they will die in a known manner within a tightly banded window of time by reviewing an immutable life in retrospect and contemplating the meaning of nonexistence.

It is a process of learning to accept that the life lived up to that point is all there is and all there ever will be. There will be no opportunity to add to it, to embellish and enhance the memories of times long past by adding new ones, no chance to redirect one's life to a different purpose or in a different direction. One can only accept that what was lived defines their existence and death will mark the end of it.

From her work with terminally ill patients grappling with this stark realization Kübler-Ross was able to observe and document a series of sequential stages of grief adaptation, emotional and psychological waypoints on the journey to death. Initially there is denial of the inevitable, followed by anger with one's circumstance, a period of bargaining, then depression and ultimately acceptance. This is, of course, an idealized representation of the process. Those facing death can become fixated at any stage never progressing beyond it. By the same token the lives of some can be truncated by death before they have time to travel the full road to acceptance.

But for those fortunate enough to come to the point of acceptance of the universal and profound truth of existence that life will surely end, a state of calm and readiness for death is the reward. At this point Kübler-Ross suggests that patients are preoccupied with completing their "unfinished business" by wrapping up loose ends so they will be able to die in peace.

Nothing as hackneyed as a "bucket list" of things a person wants to do or the exotic places they want to visit before they die, a concept that has turned dying into competition, an end-of-life game of one-upmanship, by creating a morbid scorecard for the status obsessed. It is more often small acts of letting go and saying goodbye.

Kübler-Ross gives numerous examples from her professional career of patients who need to take care of something of utmost importance for them or to accomplish a goal laden with symbolism before they can die peacefully. Little gifts, mementoes and acts such as asking for and being given permission by loved ones to die, bequeathing ordinary yet immeasurably valuable possessions to others who will appreciate them, or accomplishing a last act of liberation such as walking unassisted or a child riding a bike for the first time. The need to take care of unfinished business can be so strong that it seems to sustain life until it is done in many cases. Once the goal is reached, the affairs put in order, death can come with remarkable quickness.

Certainly the stages enumerated by Kübler-Ross describe in a general sense the landmarks passed by anyone who has confronted death and their own mortality. Denial, anger, depression and acceptance were all emotions that dominated my recovery at certain times. But I found the process to be less sequential or discrete. One psychological state did not morph into the next in a predictable trajectory toward acceptance in any way I could discern. My emotions were more apt to be comingled, to occur simultaneously as I flipped back and forth between several with one being prominent at any particular time. It was not uncommon for me to be in denial, angry and depressed on any given day.

The process I went through seemed to have two overarching phases. The first was dominated by the preoccupation with all things physical and the search for an answer to the basic question "Will I die?" and later "Will I recover?" It was not at first a certainty by any means that I would survive. Even after hospitalization and stabilization on Coumadin I did not let myself believe for a time that I was safe from another pulmonary embolism. Denial of the severity of the emergency and the magnitude of the injury caused by my slim escape from death was my primary defense in the first stage.

In the first few weeks, perhaps two months in total, after the attack matters of health were paramount. I did not think about the future or what the significance of my vascular accident could be for my life going forward. I was too preoccupied with trying to heal, of continuing in the here and now to worry about the future. I was transfixed by every physical symptom that might answer the question "Will I die?" and the search for causes of my misfortune. If a cause could be found for the DVT's and PE I would be better able to assess the likelihood that another could happen without warning and kill me and I would be able recognize the premonitory signs before it did. My superstitions were such that I was unwilling to give up on this dismal view lest something happen just as I was no longer vigilant.

I entered the second phase when it became clear that I would live and potentially for a long time, perhaps even to an age I might have expected without the traumatic attack. At that point the contemplation of how I wanted to live my life, what was important to me and if there was any solace to be had in belief in a higher power began. The anxiety I felt then was that I would not take advantage of the opportunity my near miss had provided. During this period I passed through several stages which, although similar to those identified by Kübler-Ross, were subtly different.

Not unlike the anger described by Kübler-Ross I was angry about my predicament. My anger found expression as a sense of victimization, the need to find someone responsible for my condition and to seek retribution. There was also an appeal to the supernatural or perhaps better described as a searching for beliefs in the supernatural that could explain the meaning of life and its antithesis, death. An intellectual grazing on various religious beliefs to see if any could help me deal with the fears evoked by my own mortality that had been demonstrated so convincingly to me on the beach one Saturday morning. And there was the act of winnowing, a stripping of life, love, work to their essential and irreducible forms. The drive to get rid of the daily clutter, to see the signal in the noise. A penetrating focus on the remaining time I had and how I wanted to spend it, identifying the activities and people I enjoyed and derived satisfaction from.

Between the two phases was my moment of truth. The point of complete emotional collapse when the defenses I erected to protect myself while I lived in paralyzing fear of another PE could no longer be sustained and came crashing down leaving the raw emotional core beneath. From this point of abject emotional vulnerability it was possible to move forward to redirect my life.

Hitting Bottom

Keeping the façade of normalcy erect became increasingly difficult with time. It took more and more effort to inflate the balloon that was my ego, which surrounded me with a protective shield of defenses that kept my emotions in check and people at bay. Socially the trick was not to look like a whiner, a complainer or someone who gave up, but rather as someone who sucked it up, carried on despite everything that had happened and suffered in silence.

In the early going I relied on a small set of powerful defenses to keep my ego intact. Most significant and useful was denial – the ability to compartmentalize the dangers and once contained trivialize them or simply ignore their existence. Projection – the permission to attribute the causes and consequences of my condition to others and was the prime component of my feelings of victimization. Stoicism – allowed me to keep an air of aloof detachment, dictated in large part by PTSD, one that inadvertently conveyed a tough guy image to others. Fatalism – an unwillingness to expect anything but the worst, so as not to have expectations for the future and feelings of misplaced hope. A defense made more socially palatable when seasoned well with gallows humor. In the course of time the protective utility of all defense mechanisms, these and others, diminished with over use.

But a catharsis was in the offing. An emotional reckoning that would give lie to all the bravado and nonchalance I projected. The pressure to Stay Calm and Carry On became too great and the dam against the uncontrolled flood of my emotions was bound to burst eventually. It did, spewing forth new feelings I could not contain or give voice to. They just bubbled up from the dark depths of my psyche, unprocessed sewage of my mind. It would take months to clean up the mess but without question it was the most productive part of my recovery because it allowed me to break free of the past and the person I was in it and to go forward to start a new life and make a new me.

Leaks in the dam that held my emotions in check were the first signs of the impending crisis. I noticed that increasingly I had trouble controlling my feelings and that they were becoming more labile and extreme. Thoughts, memories, stories in the news, dramas, passages in books, any stimulus I could empathize with even from the most unlikely sources could unexpectedly make me nostalgic and maudlin, revealing the fault lines in my seemingly implacable demeanor. I would tear up at the oddest and least appropriate times. My voice would crack when relating a story of something that happened to me, I had seen on television, the internet or read in a newspaper. I would have to stop mid story to regain my composure and prevent further embarrassment. I even learned to let go, to cry, when no one was around to witness my weakness. As a person who always needed to be in control and had trouble expressing emotions this was deeply disturbing.

Typically the stimuli that would set me off were directly or indirectly related to my condition. Someone who experienced misfortune through no fault of their own were apt to send me off on a jag of sentimentality. Tragedies that befell innocent children, cruelty, injury or death, were especially difficult to process. Something as simple as hearing the words to songs from Les Miserables, my favorite musical, would cause me to emote uncontrollably. The literary and musical masterpiece of heroic times, love lost and found, persecution and redemption never ceased to bring me to tears. Not only did it dramatize many of the emotions I was wrestling with it, but also made me grieve for the life that I had not lived. My life was ordinary and prosaic by comparison with the lives of characters in the play. There was nothing heroic about my existence, no great chances taken, risking all for a cause. I punished myself for my past of timidity and longed to have lived during tumultuous times.

But all this was just the prelude to the main event. I will never forget the day I hit bottom. I was the most significant day of my life. I was sitting at the dinner table with my wife and daughter. As I looked at them I was overwhelmed with how much they meant to me. What I felt was a jumbled tangle of emotions, elation that I could still be with them, gratitude for their unwavering support, the need to express how I felt to them, how inadequate an expression of my feelings would be, how ineffectively I could articulate what I was feeling. I tried to put it all together into words and just fell apart instead.

The words would not come out. Nothing but a sob-stifled noise. My daughter and wife looked at me with the anguish that must have reflected my own. We rose simultaneously – me to escape, them to comfort me. We embraced as we met. Words were hopelessly inadequate, touch was the only expression I could provide for the unfathomable love and limitless thanks I felt. We held hands and cried together. It was for me a cathartic release of all I was holding back. I surrendered to their love unconditionally. To trust that they would accept the broken me. To hope my family would not lose patience or their tempers when I was difficult or complained or when the restrictions on my life restricted theirs. That they would love me despite it all. Their touch assured me they would.

I imagine this is what alcoholics will recognize as "hitting bottom" the necessary precursor to fundamental life change. The defenses I relied on were shattered. They were crystalline and fragile anyway and not likely to hold. Nothing remained of my inner psychic fuel, I could not keep the ego preserving defenses up any more. The stuff of ego imploded like a dying star. There was nothing left of my own resources with which to carry on. The old me was not capable of meeting the exigencies of my illness.

I had my epiphany – I could not recover alone. I had to reach out for help. I was the addict surrendering to a power higher than himself, in my case the power of the love of my family. It was a transformative moment. So gut wrenching yet so cleansing I cannot relive it without tearing up, even as I write these words. From that point on I began to go forward with a new purpose, to rebuild and reshape the person I was. At the time I did not know where it would lead. I only knew that a door to the past had been closed forever.

Death and Dying vs. Life and Living

The process I underwent after hitting bottom was nearly a mirror image of the one Dr. Kübler-Ross's patients go through. There was some life audit, taking stock of who I was, how I had gotten that way, and how I would like to change. But beyond that there was a need to focus on what I wanted to become and accomplish, in short what I wanted the remainder of my life to be. Nothing as quotidian as a "midlife crisis". I did not want to go back and relive my youth. I wanted to go forward and make a new future for myself.

Rather the process involved the shedding of unfinished business that was no longer relevant, deciding instead what was truly significant in my life and letting the other things, once firmly held, fall away. It was an adaptation not to the prospect and consequences of impending death and nonexistence but instead the prospect of living with a newly imposed perception of existence and the possibility of creating a future that deviates sharply from the past. Driving me was an acute sense that my remaining time to live was finite and it could be ended in an instant. Accompanying this was an anxiety to make the most of every moment, to fill each day as full as possible. The question was: With what?

In the end what distinguishes my journey and I think that of others who have survived a life threatening event from the journey of terminal patients to death described by Dr. Kübler-Ross is one of orientation. Death is closed ended. One can only contemplate the past and one cannot change it. For the survivor of an event that nearly took their lives, the process of recovery is open-ended. There is a future of indefinite duration, a second chance filled with promise and potential. It is as if while traveling in the vehicle that is our life, the terminally ill are viewing it in the rear view mirror while the survivors of a near fatal medical emergency are looking through the windshield.

The distinction was driven home for me when in the midst of my consuming introspection about the life ahead, I received a beacon from the distant past. Early one summer afternoon a few months after the first PE, I walked to the mailbox at the end of the drive to retrieve the day's correspondence. There among the catalogs, letters and third class recyclables was an industrial strength brown envelope, the kind with a metal clasp that can be bent in opposite directions to keep it closed. It was hand addressed in large, bold print but the letters and numbers were strangely not uniform giving the outer envelope a suggestion that a ransom demand might lie within.

I opened it. Inside were a few tokens of my modest accomplishments from long before, an undergraduate diploma, athletic letter from college and few other items that would only have significance for me. Mementoes of life's small achievements from decades earlier. In the envelope stuck among the trophies was a letter from the woman who had been my wife for nine years, seven of trying and two of divorcing, three decades before. It was only the second contact I had received from her in the interim, the other being a brief telephone call.

The first paragraph read:

> *For decades, I've been meaning to return the diplomas to you. You probably don't miss them, but it's a loose end that really should be tied up. Unfortunately, this is the time when it needs to be done.*

She went on to explain she had cancer and she was entering the final phase of the disease. She assured me that her approaching death was not the disappointment that one would assume but she actually viewed it as a relief. A quick précis of her life followed, the professional accomplishments for which she expressed pride that were offset by the inability to form a lasting personal relationship. She expressed regret that our marriage had not succeed yet recognized that it ended with grace, without animosity, and hence honorably. Finally, she wished peace, comfort and joys for me and my family.

The letter could have been a case study in *On Death and Dying*. It was written by a person who had clearly reached a point of acceptance that death was imminent and that it would be a release from a battle, both personal and medical, she no longer cared to wage. There too was the need to complete unfinished business by returning items that were only valuable because of their symbolic significance, to tie up loose ends as she said. On closing she wanted to say goodbye and wished me well averring that our time together was the highpoint of her life. It was a beautiful and magnanimous expression of her love and loss, a simple, pure act of closure.

I should have left it at that but instead I immediately wrote my ex-wife. Until I received the letter I was completely unaware that she had cancer. I wanted to learn more about her condition and determine what help, if any, I could offer. The exchange of emails that followed were brutally frank and honest. The end of life needs she spoke about were so basic, so human they took my breath away and filled me with deep sorrow for her predicament. She wanted to know that she had not been forgotten, to know I harbored no anger or ill will toward her because of her behavior during our years together, to assure herself that I had meant something to her and she would not be forgotten by me after her death. What she wanted most was to re-establish our relationship in some way. She recalled the minutest details of our marriage and had obviously replayed the memories many times and interpreted them in a vacuum often. It was more creepy than flattering when I realized that I was her unfinished business.

As the conversation lengthened, spanning a period of six months, it became abundantly clear that my former wife was struggling mightily with very basic questions about the life she had lead. There was an effort on her part to reconcile the actions she had taken and their consequences, weighing what she perceived to be failures against an inventory of attributes and accomplishments in which she had pride. Creating a life's balance sheet if you will.

Chief among her self-identified failures was the inability to form a lasting intimate relationship and most specifically for the collapse of our marriage. This was offset incompletely by professional accomplishments, e.g., her personal integrity as a truth-teller in the workplace and her characterization of herself as having heroically battled against cancer, a disease that for her was in its third and last recurrence. All were reasons to feel good about herself, areas where she excelled and exceeded expectations, times and personality traits that gave her satisfaction and pride to offset the sense of failure, and accompanying shame and guilt she felt in personal relationships.

The weight she carried was the offsetting failure in personal relationships. Especially the collapse of our marriage for which she took full responsibility, over my repeated objections. From my perspective we had been in love when we married, both of us had tried to make it work over a difficult seven years but ultimately we could not. I saw no shame or guilt in that for either of us. We married for the right reasons, I thought, and had made every effort to sustain the relationship. We were both responsible for the dissolution of the marriage in my opinion or more precisely there was no fault on either of our parts. No matter how often I returned to this theme she could not accept its validity, instead steadfastly insisting on shouldering all the guilt.

The internal struggle and that lack of an acceptable resolution to the conflict was tearing her apart and preventing her from achieving the inner peace that could mark her last days. Reading this play out over numerous emails gave me a new appreciation not only of for the work Kübler-Ross's but also that of developmental psychologist Erik Erikson. Erikson was interested in human development from the standpoint of personal identity and socialization. To examine these issues, Erikson used the stages outlined in Freud's theory for psychosexual development as a point of departure and expanded on it in two important ways.

Freud was primarily interested in psychosexual development from which he hypothesized that all the psychological problems, psychoses and neuroses, originated. Psychosexual development occurred early in childhood according to Freud, before the age of 6. A child passed through three stages of development from birth to age six: initially the Oral stage from 0 to 18 months, the Anal stage from 18 months to three years old and the Phallic stage from three years to six years. There followed two stages of lesser importance: the Latency period from 6 year to puberty, roughly 12 years old, and the Genital stage extending from puberty on. Successfully navigating the early stages would enable a person to form normal sexual relationships and personality in later life, during the Genital stage. Whereas fixation in any stage would be a harbinger of psychological problems later on.

Erikson's theory enlarged the scope of Freud's framework from just psychosexual development to the broader notion of psychosocial development. Erikson was interested in the broader question: How does a person become a functioning member of society? Rather than the more limited question: How will an individual reach functional sexual relationships in adulthood? As an example of the difference, both theorists define a first stage of development and agree that it occurs between birth and about 18 months of age. Both agree that during this time a child is preoccupied with suckling and feeding. For Freud this is the Oral stage where an infant derives pleasure from oral stimulation. Fixation at this stage (continuing to gain pleasure from oral stimulations) can manifest itself in later life as excessive behaviors such as smoking, drinking and over eating. Personality traits associated with early oral fixation in turn include being unusually gullible and dependent on others. Conversely, a child who derived too little pleasure during the Oral stage could become overly pessimistic in later life.

By comparison Erikson saw this stage more generally as a period of infancy during which a child will develop an outlook on life that will assure their assimilation into social life as they got older. In this case the over-arching developmental attribute that can be internalized in this stage is Hope. The acquisition of a hopeful personality occurs, Erikson maintains, as a result of the interplay between polar opposite 'approaches to life, Trust vs. Mistrust. If during infancy a child receives affection and reliable care that satisfies their needs, the child will grow up with a sense of trust, if not, they will be generally mistrustful. The remaining stages are conceptualized in a similar manner, with a developmental goal or capacity that can be obtained through a struggle between positive and negative expressions of the goal.

Erikson's second great innovation was to extend Freud's stages beyond childhood, in fact, through the entire life course. Latency became for Erikson a period of resolving an Industry vs. Inferiority dichotomy in order to develop Competence, as an example. Erikson separated post puberty development into four age-related stages, effectively dividing Freud's Genital stage into four parts. Adolescence, from ages 12 to 18, was a time to gain a sense of self in social relationships; Young Adulthood, from 19 to 40, was a time of forming intimate bonds; Middle Adulthood, 40 to 65, creating a life's legacy through work and parenting, and most germane for my interaction with my former wife, Maturity, 65 years old to death.

Erikson conceptualized the last stage of life as one of reflection where one looks back on their lives and comes to a general assessment of how they lived and what they accomplished. In the process there is a dynamic tension between the diametric opposites, Ego Integration vs. Despair. Accomplishments, feelings of satisfaction and fulfillment lead to a satisfaction with one's life, Ego Integration, while perceived failures and disappointments lead to the belief that one has wasted their life, Despair. If successfully resolved the state reached is Wisdom, according to Erikson, a feeling akin to having a fundamental understanding of life or insight about it.

When you are in an undergraduate Psychology survey course, Erikson's theories seem very remote, detached from the life you lead, just a series of points to be memorized for the midterm. They seem to be idealized visions made of whole cloth, about what life should be some day not necessarily reflective of what it will prove to be. But as I continued the dialogue with my former wife the applicability and accuracy of Erikson's description of the challenges embedded in the last stage of life came back to me from the deep recesses of my memory because they explained with remarkable accuracy the process she and I were going through.

At times my former wife spoke from a place of Ego Integration – challenges met, contributions made, integrity shown in times that required moral and ethical values. Other messages were filled with Despair – that the marriage had failed, her implacable need to take full responsibility. She spoke too of self-censoring that lead to chances not taken and a life not as full as it could have been, and most importantly coming to this realization too late. Learning to dance just as the music ends as she put it. I feared she would never resolve her Ego Integration vs. Despair conflict. It would take a final act of acceptance, to appreciate the person she had been and let the Ego Integration win out.

I could accept that we never would have made a happy and lasting couple. She could not. There was always the sense on her part that had she been ready for marriage, more mature, our life together would have been different. Conversely I had come to terms with my conclusion decades before and that decision lead to my willingness to dissolve the marriage. I was satisfied that I had given every effort to maintaining and sustaining our relationship, as had she, but I would never be able to provide all that she needed. I resolve my guilt for my shortcoming, left it behind decades before and moved on.

Her wish to have taken more chances during her lifetime resonated with me on a fundamental level given the kinds of emotions and forward looking thoughts I was having. The point was not lost on me – live so you have no regrets when you die. Undoubtedly an impossibility but a good guiding principle nonetheless. What stayed with me as I looked through the windshield of life was the need to evaluate opportunities and weigh choices in anticipation of how I would feel when it was my turn to see life in the rearview mirror. I saw what a life ending in despair could be like, harrowingly remorseful. I still had time to understand and accept myself for all my past failures and live differently in a new life. This was not ego run amok, not a selfish, solitary pursuit of hedonic gratification. It was a quest to define the philosophical underpinnings of my life, the values and beliefs that would guide me to a life that was satisfying and fulfilling such that when I was on the verge of death I would know I had not wasted my life.

Ultimately I could not give my former wife what she need so badly – the intimacy and love we once shared. When she recognized this she decided to break off our correspondence for a period of time. We parted a second time with my promise that her memory would be safe with me while I lived. My feelings of empathy for her fate to face death alone without a person of intimacy to share it with haunts me and no doubt always will.

Relationships

My former wife's last and most meaningful gift was to show me what it will be like at the end of my life. To reveal the kinds of questions I will put to myself then and the kind of evaluation I am apt to do to in order to draw a comprehensive assessment of how I had lived. Her experience provided powerful motivation for me to navigate my life according to the standard of whether I would be able to view the sum of my existence from a position of ego integration when the end approached. Moreover, if I could not do so now, her example convinced me of the urgent need to address the matter before it was too late.

Two important elements in this regard were to understand what I wanted to do for the reminder of my life and who I wanted to do it with. With the amount of time left to me uncertain, I felt an imperative to discard the extraneous aspects of my life and concentrate on the activities that gave me the most fulfillment. To winnow the options, to pare them down to the essentials, to the ones that were consistent with my values and beliefs. So I could devote time and attention to the activities and relationships that were most gratifying.

In some ways winnowing was a conscious and deliberate effort to take charge of what was happening any way. For a host of reasons there is I think a natural tendency for a person to draw into themselves after a life threatening experience. On a physiological level it is not more complicated than the need to devote all one's physical resources to healing. For several months after the vascular accident I had no energy to do anything other than try to regain my equilibrium and re-establish a measure of stability. I was deeply wounded. I needed to hunker down and marshal my depleted resources toward getting well.

In the first few weeks my breathing was labored to the point that the simple act of taking in air, an action that had never crossed my mind until I could not do it, took physical and mental effort. Day after day of working twenty-five times a minute or more to fill my lungs with gasping breaths left me exhausted while operating on less than optimal blood oxygen levels left me physically and mentally weak. In addition during the first few months following release from the hospital I had very little stamina. Walking for any appreciable distance proved daunting. Serious exercise was out of the question. That was a given. But the lack of stamina also affected my willingness and ability to engage in social activities. By the end of the day I was too exhausted to consider anything that required additional effort, socializing or something as simple as going to a movie for example.

Reaction to a new powerful drug regimen added its own set of complications. My daily dose of Coumadin not only had an immediate, admittedly beneficial, impact on my physical functioning but by extension to my mental status as well. Most noticeable was a precipitous drop in blood pressure, from high normal, 140 over 90, to below target levels for a healthy adult, 115 over 70. There was a concomitant drop in my heart rate from the mid 70's beats per minute rate to the low 50's. Overall this caused a calming even soporific effect. I was so mellow I drank copious quantities of coffee to regain the level of mental acuity I had enjoyed before my medical woes began. Road rage was a thing of the past.

After a few months the physical indications of my injury began to subside. The need to stay withdrawn did not however. Thereafter it was driven by the need to adjust to my new place in the social milieu. Having a life threatening medical emergency changes a person's relationships to family and social world, I found. As I emerged from my hermitlike cocoon it was not easy to pick up where I had left off even had I wanted to. I had to feel my way along, testing each relationship to see where to begin. Sorting through these new perceptions and interactions was unmapped territory. I was feeling my way along trying to gauge where I stood, taking my cues from the actions of others.

Interacting with my immediate family, friends and colleagues during the recovery required constant adjustment and modification of old patterns. With respect to my immediate family, in many ways they had been through a parallel process to mine. They were tense and frightened, unsure of the prognosis and in a situation over which they could exercise very little control. The prospect that I might die was just as real for them and it was for me. In the very early going as I lay in the hospital my wife and daughter spent their nights, when they were not with me, devouring whatever information they could find on the internet, in order to understand what had happened to me and what they could expect over the near and long term. My son wanted to come home immediately and called multiple times a day to get updates. Knowledge was power, a means of regaining some semblance of control over events which were inherently uncontrollable.

As time progressed, I was not the only one who needed to release all the pent up tension. This lead to several, what I felt were unprovoked, arguments wherein I was taken to task on a variety of issues. While I interpreted this as blaming the victim, I am sure I provided ample reason for the disagreements. The behavioral matches that set off the explosions were typically mundane however. In fact, I suspect that any provocation would have set off the blow-ups. My family needed to express their frustrations with the situation in which we all found ourselves, ones they repressed until it was safe to do so in deference to my illness and precarious health.

My wife too was going through a process of winnowing, trying to decide how she wanted to spend the rest of her life and where. We often differed on what our priorities were. We had different visions of the future. There was talk of going our own way several times punctuated with compromises and the melding of our visions. It remains an ongoing adjustment process.

It was difficult for me to be faced with unreasoning anger when I felt I should be getting sympathy instead. In the case of my children, I gained some perspective into their thinking as I recalled a period when I too seemed to be constantly angry and dismissive of my father, a person I idolized throughout my life. I knew those feeling were coming from within me not because of some objective thing he was doing. It took considerable time to solve the puzzle of my actions toward him. I was angry because he was getting older and exhibiting signs of aging. The person I grew up with, who always seemed invincible, now was very much vulnerable. He was slower, more stooped, weakened – he was getting old and I was mad at him on a subconscious level for letting it happen. I wondered if my children were sensing the same thing in me and reacting the same way. I had proven the fallacy of my physical invincibility quite dramatically after all.

It hurt, I admit, to be diminished in their eyes and esteem. I would never again be the go-to source for advice on every topic again for them. I would no longer be the sagacious voice of experience they sought out. But as I had with my father they would transition to more prominent roles in the family, eventually the dominant ones. It would have happened eventually anyway, if not in as sudden a manner, and it would have hurt all the same.

As unpleasant as the arguments could be, giving vent to the roiling emotions my family members were collectively feeling sped the healing process, I think. It allowed us all to deal with the fact that everything had changed – household responsibilities, allocation of tasks, family roles, sex, and decision-making – everything. The structure of our family, the roles we counted on for normalcy all had to be adjusted. The interactions and connections between family members would not be the same going forward and I and they needed to come to terms with the new reality.

The anger faded with time. A new normal was achieved. It was one in which I had a lesser role in the family, where my spouse and children were more assertive and made more of the decisions. Whereas before I made most of the decisions on joint activities, now many more decisions were being made without me. I for one would not be able to pick up where I left off and assume the position I held exactly as before. This took some getting used to and still does.

Extending out a bit from my nuclear family to other family members and friends, my means of coping was to withdraw almost totally from them. In the hospital I did not want to talk with anyone so we instituted a modified telephone tree where my wife spoke to one sister who in turn relayed the news and updates on my progress to the remainder of the family. Even then the news was closely held. My cousins and the last remaining person from my parent's generation, an uncle, were not included in the inner circle. To this day they know nothing of the near fatal events. I prefer it this way. I am not my vascular accident. It is not my identity.

Close friends were totally excluded as well. A friend of 40+ years, as an example, called several times, in the months after the events. Nothing special just the usually checking in. I didn't answer or return any of his calls. After perhaps the third attempt on his part, I wrote a short email and told him I had been "under the weather" and had not answered the phone responded to his messages as a consequence. I was a year and half after the first PE before I reached out to him but still withheld information about my health misadventures even then. I am certain I will never let on now.

Although I valued my anonymity and tried to preserve it, not going out at all was not an option and this brought me into contact with friends and acquaintances whether I liked it or not. Going out I gravitated to places and activities where I was unlikely to meet someone I knew or have to interact them if I did. Movies were perfect. I live in a small town and when I ran into people I knew, which was often, they would routinely ask about my health. I began to realize just how widespread the knowledge of my near miss was in the community. It was not a question of hiding my condition from them or of making people aware of what happened, they already knew.

It was annoying to have to answer questions about my health over and over again. I knew friends and acquaintances were well meaning but still I just didn't want to have to explain myself, to prove I was alright again, and signal they could interact with me as they always had. The typical accidental interrogation was best typified by the double question. "How are you feeling?" followed by an innocuous response such as "I'm doing well". Not taken at face value, a second question followed with a more sincere and imploring re-ask of this sort "Are you doing OK?" I am remind of this sequence now when I meet someone I haven't seen since the event and it is repeated again more than a year after the PE. Today it is more of a source of amusement than the annoyance it was then.

One of the things I disliked the most was having to explain to people what had happened. I got tired of telling the story, not only because it forced me to relive the details of my near miss but also because it became a repetitious and tedious chore. More accurately I got tired of evaluating the reaction of people when they heard it. There were, naturally, amazed looks as I described the events, the jaw-dropping and head-shaking reaction. There was nothing flattering or reinforcing about the reactions either. I didn't consider my behavior after the event to be brave or heroic. Quite the contrary, I thought I escaped due to pure dumb luck and I did not think that warranted any imputations of exceptionalism. To me it had the negative connotation of being a victim, someone who had been screwed by fate.

For my part the story telling was a trial and error process of trying to find the right story to tell and how to tell it, how many graphic details to include to emphasize the gravity of the situation and the good fortune of the escape, how much stoic humor to add to embellish the tough guy demeanor, while carefully gauging the audience to avoid the social faux pas of boring the listener with too much information. Mostly I just wanted to get it over without becoming the center of attention, to do or say anything that would bring the subject up. I wanted to reassimilate seamlessly.

I quickly learned that publicity of my illness changed the perceptions of me by my family and friends. I was the injured one, the damaged person who could not participate fully in activities. There were subtle changes in relationships, a simultaneous withdrawal of one from the other. After the accident others were less apt to listen to my comments, to begin to speak before I finished a sentence as if I had nothing of import to say. I felt that I had lost position in the status hierarchy, my opinion counted less and at time that I was being left behind.

Business contacts were especially problematic in this regard. Some responsibilities associated with my involvement in several companies was mandatory and nonparticipation was not an option. Additionally, there was a very different dynamic going on with business relationships, a more competitive one. Expressions of goodwill, tended to be perfunctory, gratuitous, often patronizing and even disingenuous. The interest in my medical injury was less about my health than about how the power relationships within a business would be affected.

As with all relationships, business contacts were altered by my illness, few for the better in this arena unfortunately. As an example, there is a subtle association between masculinity, size, and intellect with dominance in business. I had always benefited from the fact that I was physically imposing, 6'4" and 240 pounds. After the PE I could sense that because of my illness the natural tendency to leadership that accrued from my physical stature was reduced. Some business associates even tried to capitalize on my apparent weakness to improve their position relative to mine. These were precisely the kind of associations that were the targets for winnowing. Limiting business activities going forward or ending them if possible was motivated in large part by the fundamentally unsatisfying nature of business interactions.

Was all the withdrawal and withholding information a good strategy to deal with my illness? I believe it was. It gave me time to work things out, to get physically stronger, not to jump back into life too quickly before I was prepared. But more than that it made the re-entry into social life easier once I decided I was ready to re-engage. I did not have to deal with reactions of others or subtle changes in their perception of me. As my mother once said when I asked why she refused to tell anyone she had cancer. "They assume it is a death sentence and they write you off", she replied.

My problems didn't qualify as a death sentence as it is understood in the popular imagination but I could appreciate the point she was making. A sudden medical emergency or serious illness, just as surely as a terminal illness, changes a person's relationship with the social world – often in a way that is not positive if one wants to eventually pick up where they left off. The trick was to pick up from a different place.

Finding Purpose

The companion process to winnowing relationships was winnowing the demands on my time. Like personal interactions this involved cutting back to the essentials, to a core set of activities I enjoyed and found ego-enhancing. As I felt better I started to contemplate in earnest where I wanted to spend my time. This in turn meant letting go of everything that did not contribute to feelings of self-worth or acted against the goal of self-actualization. It meant instead going forward with new purpose to find fulfillment during the rest of my life.

At some point during the process of winnowing, I revisited every project I ever considered doing but for some forgotten reason had never gotten around to starting or finishing. There was always the lingering tug of disappointment that I had not carried though with an idea, a brilliant one in my estimation, but they all were by that standard. Now seemed like a good time to take a second look in order to make sure I had not left a meaningful project undone.

I dusted off old proposals, prospecti for books I wanted to write, research projects I considered doing, theories I once developed but had never gathered data to test. I toyed with each idea, considered alternative approaches, estimated what kind of commitment it would take and if I wanted to spend my time that way. The reassessment was quite valuable in the end, not because I found a new mission in life, but because it confirmed the conclusion I first made, that the projects should be abandoned. I could leave them behind for good now with a clear conscience.

Old hobbies and activities I might pursue got similar treatment. At one time or another in my adult life I had been an avid bird watcher, sea shell and butterfly collector. In the past I had indulged each of these avocations in different ways. For a number of years I was a docent in the local wildlife refuge where I spotted birds and interpreted their behavior for visitors. I traveled abroad to study butterflies and caught and mounted nearly every species indigenous to my island home. I collected shells from all travels. I was even motivated originally to move to Sanibel in part because it afforded me an opportunity to indulge my shell collecting and bird watching hobbies. Each of these pastimes was important to me and I would continue to enjoy them as long as I was able I was sure. But none was a compelling passion, one I wanted to immerse myself in totally or even take up with the single-mindedness I once had.

I decided instead to redouble my travel schedule now that I was able. As a sociologist by training I found cultural diversity endlessly fascinating, and sadly it was vanishing frighteningly fast. I am intrigued by the variability in beliefs and practices surrounding common human activities such as procreation, parenting, burial practices and spiritual beliefs to name a few. Additionally many of the most interesting examples of human diversity are in remote and inaccessible areas, so travel has the extra potential to satisfy my naturalist impulses. The allure of Mt. Kailash, a succinct encapsulation of these interests, was stronger than ever. Tempus fugit however. I needed to make the trips before the cultures and I were no more.

Undoubtedly the most difficult area of winnowing involved professional and business activities. As a quasi-academic I always had the intellectual desire to conduct research and to publish the results. In essence, it is a desire of mine to engage in the professional dialogue and debate in my chosen specialty, to have something to say in an area of particular interest to me. For a scientist, conjectures need to be backed up by evidence and hence the need to conduct original research and publish in peer reviewer journals, ones in which other similarly inclined and interested colleagues and not infrequently competitors, friendly or otherwise, can pass judgment on the merit of your efforts.

As I recovered, there was a part of me that wanted to continue to do research. It is enjoyable and I am good at it. With the plethora of new journals and means of publication options that are available, the opportunities to do so are numerous. Not a week goes by when I do not receive an invitation to submit a manuscript to a journal, to attend a conference as a participant, or review an article for a journal. I was sorely tempted to jump back into the fray. However, the first two options, research and conferences, usually required the collection of original data, something I had neither the time nor inclination or resources to accomplish. Moreover as the first article I ever published approached its 40th anniversary in print plus all the articles, chapters, and books I published since, there is little one more article can do for my career, which if I were to evaluate it objectively, is in decline.

But my knowledge of a field and the literature in it remained strong and still had value. So I opted to continue as an editorial referee for selected journals in my field. In this way I could assess the merits of new papers and influence the direction of the field. It was a good compromise. I could stay active professionally, to have my say while helping to support and continue the scientific process I respect. The solution I reached in my professional life was perhaps the most successful example of winnowing I have. It was just the right combination personal interest tempered by the reality of my capabilities while giving me a chance to remain productive.

One thing that always weighed on my mind in this regard was how I had used, or more correctly not used, the last degree I received, a master's degree in public health. I came to public health late in life at the age of 56. Before that I had a successful and gratifying career in market and advertising research. After 30 years the personal and professional benefits that accrued from continuing along the same well-worn path were minimal. I was stagnating, doing the same types of studies, learning little new. I itched for a change. Public health was the choice. My goal was to work with my consulting clients in a new way, to help them address the public health issues specific to their businesses, e.g., to work with alcoholic beverage companies to address the effect of advertising on adolescent drinking or with the NFL to reduce football injuries at all levels of play. After graduation I tried to do just that. I spent the next three years proving that public health was not a concern of business or I was not the one to convince them of its importance – probably both.

But I was still a public health professional. My original idea was a failure – a noble failure I liked to believe – but I could still make a contribution to the field. Then out of the blue it hit me – right in the chest, as a matter of fact. As I began to try to understand my illness, I realized that near fatal medical emergencies were a major hidden public health problem, not just for the person who suffered the attack, but for their families, and the medical community as well. The PTSD I experienced was just becoming recognized as a by-product of near fatal accidents and serious medical procedures. Meanwhile very little was now about the basic epidemiology of PE's. Morbidity and mortality figures were just guess work. It seemed to me that near death medical problems generally and PE's in particular provided a wealth of possibilities to continue to be productive in public health.

Initially, I was struck by the similarities between the kinds of feelings and adjustment stages that I was experiencing and those outlined by Dr. Kübler-Ross. I decided to emulate her approach and interview survivors of PE's to see if their recovery followed a path similar to mine. Like many of my research ideas this one died of its own weight. I would never be able to duplicate an entire career even if I were as insightful and creative as Dr. Kübler-Ross. This book is the accommodation. My attempt to document what I went through as a starting point with the intent to continue researching new life experiences for the remainder of my productive life. I could not wait to start.

But first I had to wrap up a few things. I carried forward a number of business entanglements from my pre-PE life. More than that they were my life before, where I sent all my time and energy. Not the least of these was a restaurant I had started with a partner. It failed and I needed to attend to the administrative aspects of the shutdown. I owned a significant interest and was part of the supervisory management of two others. Several others were just investments, entered into for financial gain, and they were struggling in the recession. There were common threads uniting all these entanglements; they were: time consuming to monitor and manage, socially unrewarding if not aggravating, and distractions that delayed me from starting on what I really wanted to do.

My objective was to end my involvement as quickly as possible with all but one of the investments, and reduce my engagement in that one considerably. The goal, simplicity itself in conceptualization, proved easier to imagine than to effect. Some responsibilities associated with supervisory management could not be avoided and withdrawal or limiting my time in these enterprises was not an option. As much as I wanted to divest myself of my ownership in the "pure" investments there was no market for the shares and the prospects of a return on my investments looked to be slim or none. The more I tried to make something happen the deeper I got in the workings of the businesses until I was again fully committed.

Six months after almost losing my life I had come full circle. I was as deeply engaged in business as I ever had been. Working on my new interests had been put on hold. It had proven impossible to disengage from my commitments, to monetize my investments, take losses if need be, to settle accounts once and for all and to strike out in a new direction. Instead there were as many demands on my time and I was under as much stress and just as tightly wound as before.

This came home to me full force one night when I was attending the theater out of town. On the way to the performance I was on my cellphone discussing a business problem with a colleague. After the show the first thing I did was check my cellphone again to see if I have received a emails, calls or texts while the phone was silenced inside the theater. I was a thousand miles away from home and I was trying in off hours to control things from afar. My goal to simplify my life and move on to something more gratifying endeavors had completely fallen by the wayside. I needed a wake-up call to snap me out of the default mode I had slipped back into or all the insight I had gained from a breath taking flirtation with sudden death and the resulting new purpose I found in life would be lost.

The next morning the alarm went off.

CHAPTER SEVEN
RELAPSE

"Hey, if it wasn't for bad luck, y'all Oh! I wouldn't
have no luck at all."

—*Ray Charles*
(1903 – 2004)

If nothing else, bleeding to death is colorful. Or so I would find
out quite unexpectedly one morning.

Ironically the near fatal bleed out occurred exactly six
months to the day after I experienced the pulmonary embolism
that nearly killed me. Six months is generally the time the
medical community believes it takes to recovery from such an
event. By then the clots are dissolved, reabsorbed or have
adhered to the wall of a vein, becoming a permanent part of it,
and posing no more danger of breaking free and migrating to
the lungs by way of the heart. Six months also usually marks
the time that Coumadin therapy is stopped.

My personal recovery was right on schedule. All the
symptoms of venous disease were resolved. Swelling and
inflammation in the offending leg were a thing in the past.
Indications of restricted blood flow, redness, heat and pain,
were gone as well. Meanwhile my respiration was as good as it
had been before the initial event or at least was so close I did
not perceive any reduction in capacity.

I was even looking forward to a disease free, and especially
a Coumadin free future. Thoughts of taking the long delayed
trek to Mt. Kailash returned as did my penchant to spend idle

time mentally prioritizing the places I would visit and in what order. Ascending the Inca Trail, hiking Patagonia, penetrating the formidable Ruwenzori Range, the legendary Mountains of the Moon, preoccupied my thoughts. But life has a way of punishing such hubris as I was to find out – again. Or was it another warning?

Bleeding to Death

The incident began innocently enough. Over breakfast I felt the slightest trickle of wetness under my nose as if it were beginning to run on a frosty autumn morning. Absentmindedly I wiped it away only to notice that my hand came back streaked with bright red arterial blood. Not surprisingly the possibility of being at mortal risk from an out of control nosebleed did not enter my mind at this point. If it had I would have thought it laughable. This despite the fact that nosebleeds, bleeding gums, unusual bruising and other indications of proclivity to hemorrhage are signs medical professionals routinely inquire about as a part of Coumadin monitoring.

Bleeding is, of course, the most serious "side effect" of long-term therapeutic Coumadin use. Uncontrolled bleeding episodes are made all the more serious by the frequency with which they occur and the significant hazard they represent. A meta-analysis of 33 studies, involving 4,373 patients, as an example, found that major bleeding events occur between 1% and 7% per year of warfarin use and 13.4% of these cases result in death. A later and larger meta-analysis of 69 studies found that .2% of patients have a major bleeding event in the first three months of use and 11.3% die because of it.

Additionally, major bleeding from anticoagulation therapy puts a significant burden on emergency medical services. In the US Coumadin accounts for 29,000 of the 700,000 emergency room visits each year that are due to Adverse Drug Events (ADEs). Coumadin accounts for 4% of all ADEs, therefore. This figure rises by age group to 16% of emergency room visits for ADEs among those over the age of 50 and to 33% for people 65 years old or older. This clearly is a drug one disrespects at one's own peril.

I checked again. The blood was still flowing from one nostril. Using the age-old home remedy for stopping a nosebleed, I packed the nostril with tissue, applied pressure and lay down for a few minutes. The bleeding seemed to slacken and quit. I waited for a few more minutes, removed the tissue and rechecked. No further bleeding was apparent so I returned to my interrupted meal.

The next few minutes were uneventful. Then, as I was looking down at the food on my plate, a large glossy drop of bright red blood landed in the middle of it. Another followed, and another, a steady metronome of drops keeping time with the beat of my heart. The tempo increased with my rising anxiety, but even then the full gravity of the situation was lost to me.

I rushed to the bathroom and began a second round of packing. But this time as the bleeding picked up the packing saturated through almost immediately after it was inserted. Ominously blood began to drip from the other nostril. No amount of packing or pressure could stem the flow. Blood gushed whenever the packing was changed, over the sink, onto the floor, toilet water turned red from disposed tissues, white towels were spotted crimson. Quickly the scene became a chaotic panorama of blood splashes and stains as if it were the aftermath of some horrific shoot out or a Jackson Pollock study in scarlet.

This was no ordinary nosebleed. I packed the nose again, applied pressure as before and lay down. Within a minute blood stopped flowing out of my nostrils but instead began running from the back of my nose, flowing behind my palette and down my throat. The bleeding had been going on for over a half an hour by then with increasing tempo. I was making no headway in bringing it to a halt.

I needed help. I asked my wife to check where the nearest hospital emergency room was located. This being New York, we decided against calling an ambulance. Hailing a cab seemed more expedient.

By the time I boarded the cab and made the nine block drive to the hospital the blood flow became an unstoppable torrent. Blood poured from my nose. No longer a trickle it streamed down the back of my throat at the same time. I could barely breathe through the flow. I swallowed what I could, spit the rest and choked all at the same time. It was as if I were being water boarded by my own blood. Suddenly drowning seemed like a real possibility.

We arrived at St Luke's Roosevelt Hospital on New York's Upper West Side. It took an interminable ten minutes to make the nine block drive in rush hour traffic. One-way streets put the cab a block short of our goal, emergency room admitting. The cabbie volunteered to continue around the block to the entrance but I could not take it anymore so I exited the cab and walked the last block entering the reception area with a wad of blood saturated paper towels pressed over my nose and mouth.

The receptionist asked me to sign in. Drops of blood splashed on the form as I did. She then told me to take a seat in the nearly empty waiting room. Undoubtedly she saw many bleeding patients during a day but from my side of the paper towels her demeanor seemed like sangfroid to the point of callousness. I took a seat for a few minutes choking the entire time.

Envisioning a lengthy wait, something I experienced before in an ER, I returned to the reception counter, removed the paper towels and as blood splattered on the counter and floor, I said "I think they will want to see me right away". That seemed to be the Open Sesame I needed, since as she recoiled she waved an attendant over who ushered me into the triage area.

Emergency rooms are odd places existing at the edge of life and death, a portal to eternity. Strangers come in and some will pass through the portal and cease to exist. The ER and its staff are organized around determining which of the strangers delivered into their care are in immediate danger of crossing the line and preventing them from doing so if it is at all medically and humanly possible. I was in obvious distress as they began their assessment of my predicament.

The first step is to convert strangers into patients by: gathering oral information that will humanize the distress while looking for clues to its cause, taking vital signs to determine the gravity and immediacy of the stranger's condition, prioritizing the need for care and determining a course of action for those in no need of heroic measures. An ER is simply a waypoint on the journey to somewhere else, admission, release or death. The triage nurse began the interrogation to determine which path I would take.

For the next 10 minutes we tried to communicate through a spray of flying blood. What was not expectorated when I spoke poured out into the wad of paper towels I carried or dripped onto the front of the hospital gown I wore. Through the gore the nurse was able to inquire and I was able to convey very basic information, my age, history of DVTs and PEs, length of Coumadin use, dosage, the last time I took the medicine, and the fact that I had been asymptomatic until that morning, and had no previous evidence of Coumadin-related bleeding.

The interview was a struggle on both sides. Talking accelerated the bleeding. It reached the point where it became too difficult to breathe and answer questions at the same time. By an unspoken mutual agreement the nurse and I gave up and abandoned the effort to provide more details.

Thereafter I became a patient. I was assigned a room, more of a waiting area with a bed and privacy drape really, and for lack of a better description, left alone and uncared for while the medical staff practiced a seemingly "I couldn't care less" nonchalance. There was no rush to offer treatment. No checking in to see how I was doing. While this seemed infuriatingly insensitive even heartless at the time, in retrospect I see it as a strategy that allows the situation to resolve itself as many often do. Matters stabilize, get better or worse at which point the physician knows what to do next.

After a period of observation during which the bleeding slowed but ultimately showed no evidence of stopping entirely, the physician on duty intervened. Keeping up a light and reassuring banter, sotto voce he said he would try to pack my nose with a hemostatic material and in his experience that measure most often controlled the bleeding. He then took a brief leave and returned with two thin dowels, approximately six inches in length, each wrapped in a white gauze-like material that tapered to a point. He instructed me to tilt my head back whereupon he quickly inserted the wrapped dowels into the nostrils and up deep into the sinuses, an excruciating procedure that I can only liken to being lobotomized with a pencil.

But with the pain came the faith that the procedure would finally staunch the terrifying flow of blood. Any momentary pain was endurable with that expectation. Over the next 14 hours this recyclable faith in the promise of final reprieve from the bloody discharge sustained me through every intervention, each more draconian than the last. Faith that the bleeding would stop if we tried just one more technique became a convenient fiction, a matter of self-delusion that reduced pain and kept my spirits up.

This is not to say there were no glimmers of hope or moments of optimism. To the contrary the blood flow ceased on occasion as a consequence of an intervention or just as often for no apparent reason only to start again with a renewed vigor. The number of packings mounted throughout the day, blood soaked gowns were changed, catch basins of streaming and expectorated blood filled and were emptied during the futile attempt to find a solution.

But there came a point when the interventions did more damage than good. Repeated packing damaged the mucous lining of the nostril adding to the number of bleeding sites. Multiple efforts to cauterize the wounds only exacerbated the situation. Ultimately the well intentioned interventions caused so much iatrogenic damage that it was inconceivable that the bleeding could be stopped without first dealing with the underlying cause, the inability of my blood to clot caused by the anticoagulation effects of the Coumadin regimen that was protecting me from further DVTs and PEs.

The mechanics of a nosebleed or any other bleeding wound for that matter are quite simple. A barrier between the body and its environment has been breached. Blood starts to flow from the wound, which in turn activates an array of bodily defense mechanisms. White blood cells, t-cells, and other specialized blood-borne bodies rendezvous at the wound in order to find and destroy any alien organisms that could cause infection and imperil the host.

Blood plasma rich with clotting factors, most notably Vitamin K, is also present and the clotting components are able to stem the flow if the right conditions are met. Like a fire clotting begins when three conditions occur together: there is a cause – inflammation or injury; fuel is present – pooled or slow moving blood; a spark sets off the reaction. Vitamin K is the spark which when the other conditions are met causes a chain of biochemical events, a cascade as it is described by physicians, that result in coagulation of the blood and the formation of a clot.

Uncontrolled bleeding can be seen in this regard as a very simple matter of the blood flowing too fast to remain in place long enough for a wound-sealing blockage to form. Quite literally, the clotting factors get swept away with the blood loss. Hence the usual methods employed to slow the bleeding, pressure and packing, are effective because they allow the blood to pool long enough to clot. Pooling is however precisely the effect anticoagulation therapy is meant to prevent in the first place. Such is the delicate balance between stasis and crisis.

I had been asymptomatic before the event with no hints or preceding incidents to suggest that a major bleed was in the offing. My medical team and I pondered the question of what caused the mysterious and unexpected nosebleed at length in the days following the episode. Eventually we arrived at a working hypothesis. The forced hot air heating system in my apartment created a hyper-arid environment. The low humidity dried out my airway and caused the mucous membranes in my nose and sinuses to crack and bleed. The light bleeding to start was amplified by my anticoagulated state and anxiety elevated-blood pressure. Attempts to stop the flow with packing had the opposite effect until the bleeding reached a tipping point where the speed of the bleeding was faster than the time it took my slow clotting blood to create a wound sealing clot.

When I entered the emergency room my INR level was 3.3 i.e., it took me 3.3 times as long to form a clot as a normal person. Although high for me the reading is not abnormally high. Patients with some common diseases such as atrial fibrillation have a target INR range of 2.5-3.5. No doubt exacerbating this was that I also took a "baby" aspirin (81mg) daily to protect against arterial clotting and my blood pressure was abnormally high for me (155 over 97) when I arrive at the ER.

Whatever the reasons behind it, the blood flowed freely from both nostrils. For the next 14 hours I was subjected to intervention after intervention, packing and repacking, injections and ultimately a blood transfusion, all intended to slow the bleeding sufficiently to allow a clot time to form.

The packing inserted by the ER physician seemed to work initially. Bleeding slowed and no longer ran down the back of my throat. For an hour I rested, progressively relaxing. The more time passed the more it appeared that the problem was solved. Then I decided to relieve myself, stood and walked to the restroom, my bloody gown drawing interested stares from the other patients. But standing must have increased my blood pressure enough to reverse the balance between the rate of blood flow and my body's ability to form clots. Menacingly blood started to trickle from my nose. By the time I returned to my draped cubicle, the blood was flowing full force and I was once again choking on it.

This one-act drama would be repeated numerous times throughout the day and into the night. An intervention would be tried. It would appear to be successful. Within an hour, often associated with standing and walking, the bleeding would return with a vengeance.

Unable to staunch the bleeding the ER doctor passed me to the Ear Nose and Throat (ENT) specialists. A call upstairs summoned an ENT Physician's Assistant (PA) who upon arrival removed the packing with what I can only describe as a sadistic yank. He then replaced the packing with a second, wider set of nostril tampons and shoved them up my nose and deeper into my sinuses, confirming to me his sadistic tendencies. The pain was beyond belief. I was convinced I was in the Cuckoo's Nest and this Big Nurse was intent on obliterating my prefrontal cortex sans anesthesia.

Again, there followed a brief respite during which I tried to breathe with two satay skewers protruding from my nose, with temples throbbing, eyes watering and while the PA de Sade did paperwork. But as before, the rest was fleeting. The blood with no exit path through my nostrils dripped, trickled and then ran in torrents down my throat. I coughed splattering my gown with crimson diadems, swallowed what I could and spit the rest – what seemed to me to be gallons of blood – into a catch basin. Remarkably all this time the thought that I could be anything more than uncomfortable didn't enter my mind. It was just too inconceivable that I could die of a nosebleed given the more significant maladies I had dodged.

Admitting defeat, the PA arranged to have me transferred upstairs to the ENT clinic. The waiting room was full when I arrived. The occupants recoiled at the sight of a wheel-chaired patient in the blood stained gown with the bloody towel pressed to his face. I was put in an examination room immediately and the specialist, PA, nurse and MD in training came in. Over the next four hours, my nose was packed and unpacked at least three times. Visible bleeding sites were cauterized multiple times and at least that was successful in closing the wound in the right nostril. However, the offending vessels in the left side were too high in the sinuses to be reached and cauterized.

And all the while, the blood flowed. At times gowns were changed every 20 minutes. Spit basins changed more frequently. Talking was impossible. At some point we crossed a line where the interventions stopped being therapeutic and began to exacerbate the bleeding. And yet there was always one more technique to try, hemostatic tape, cauterization, packing, and so on without end. The pain was nearly unbearable and finally when the physician suggested that we try a balloon to block the affected nostrils I threw in the towel. I refused any further treatment.

When the specialist tried to convince me to go on, arguing that he was trying to keep me out of surgery, I decided to address the elephant in the room. Although no one had addressed causes, it was obvious to anyone who knew my history that while Coumadin did not start the bleeding, once started Coumadin was responsible for it continuing. The next step was quite apparent to me. The Coumadin effect had to be reversed by an administration of Vitamin K. The physicians reluctantly agreed and back to the ER we went, terrorizing a new set of waiting room patients on the way.

Despite all its drawbacks, the inconvenience and trading one set of risks for another set, Coumadin has many advantages. In addition to being the least expensive anticoagulant medicine on the market, it has been in use for over half a century administered on an acute and long-term basis to millions of individuals. As a consequence, the protocols for Coumadin treatment are finely calibrated for every condition and indication.

But there is one other characteristic of Coumadin that makes it indispensable in situations like the one I faced. Its effect is reversible. The anticoagulation effect can be neutralized to the point it has no effect at all and a person's clotting capability returns to that of a normal individual. This fail-safe option does not act immediately but it does occur in time to prevent exsanguination. The option is not to be used frivolously or indiscriminately but only as a last resort because rapidly crashing one's INR can create hazards in its own right as I found out.

When I returned to the ER another battery of blood tests were administered. While we waited for the results the attending physicians attempted to estimate the amount of blood loss. This exercise was intended to determine how many units of blood I would receive by transfusion. Two liters of blood loss is considered a "serious" bleed offset by a transfusion of two units of clotting agents whereas when the bleed is life-threatening time is of the essence and four units are administered. The consensus guess among the physicians was I had lost in excess of two liters.

Whatever the actual number, the blood tests revealed that by every measure of essential blood components – red blood cells, white cells, platelets, hemoglobin and hematocrit (percentage of blood made up of red blood cells) – had dropped 30-40% since I was admitted to the ER 10 hours earlier. I experienced a 40% blood loss with no evidence that it would not continue. Values that were on the high side of normal earlier in the day were now below the lowest boundaries of the normal range. Simply put, I was slowly bleeding to death.

The average person has approximately 5 liters of blood. Blood loss of 50% or greater is the threshold beyond which a person is likely to go into shock and exsanguination quickly becomes irreversible. I was approaching the threshold. The nurses and attending physician asked repeatedly if I was cold, the first sign of shock. More people were engaged in treating me now and their concern seemed to increase perceptibly.

Blood was ordered and while we waited for it to arrive the specialist in charge tried yet one more intervention. This time the intervention was an injection of anesthesia in the upper palate in the hope that it would slow arterial blood flow to the affected area. I was choking on the blood running down my throat to such a degree that it took multiple tries to complete the injections.

Another major concern discussed was that I would not be able to digest all the blood I had swallowed. So I was given an anti-nausea drug through the IV. It had the opposite effect – although I often wonder if what happened was actually the desired effect. I began almost immediately to vomit huge quantities of blood violently and uncontrollably. Rushing to a nearby sink to vomit, I struck my head on the sharp edge of an overhanging cabinet. Imagine the site; a person leaning over a sink, blood streaming from a cut across his forehead, pouring out of his nose, while he retched violently and projectile vomited gore. It was a scene out of Quentin Tarantino's imagination.

Eventually the blood plasma needed to reverse the Coumadin effect arrived and the first bag was hung on the delivery tree. The transfusion consisted of bags holding a yellowish fluid. I was told it was fresh frozen plasma (FFP) fortified with Vitamin K as opposed to whole blood since FFP contained the needed clotting factors.

Giving blood products to a person is no small matter and is only done as an absolute necessity. Transfused blood can carry with it blood-borne viruses such as Hepatitis C and HIV. While screening for those pathogens reduces the risk of infection it can fail and in the case of HIV since the incubation period of the disease prevents its detection for several weeks after it is contracted by the blood donor. Other risks involve possible rejection of the transfused blood, reactions to antibodies in it, and adverse reaction to the mechanics of the transfusion.

Under the circumstances physicians warn the patient of the risks involved, make sure they understand them and gain the patient's consent. The physician in charge went over all of this with me in a solemn manner. It was not unlike receiving the Last Rites on a battlefield. You are in no position to say no.

Over the next half hour I was transfused with two units of FFP. Immediately I began to rest easier sure in the expectation that the Coumadin would soon be neutralized and that my body's natural abilities would again be able to stop the bleeding. In retrospect, it is somewhat remarkable to realize that never throughout the process was I actually in fear for my life. I always assumed that if the worst transpired, my INR could be brought back in line and I could be sustained if necessary with transfusions of whole blood in the interim.

My discomforts were instead much more immediate and far less apocalyptic. I was in pain, not acute stabbing pain as I had been sporadically throughout the day but a general soreness in my face, behind my eyes, in my throat, but also aching in my shoulders, back and head from bracing against the therapeutic interventions and in my abdomen and diaphragm from the convulsive vomiting. Although I had not eaten anything of note for nearly 24 hours I was not hungry, as a result of being sustained by the ingestion and digestion of my own blood. More than anything else I was simply worn out and wanted it all to end.

The bleeding had slackened for a moment as it did inexplicably over the course of the day. I sat perfectly still. Even the simple act of talking or answering the physician's questions could restart the torrential flow. To prevent this from happening while we waited for the Vitamin K to kick in (6-24 hours), the ENT specialist packed my nose one more time. I learned later, that she crammed six feet of hemostatic tape into my left nostril alone. This mass was the rough equivalent of having a Ping-Pong ball up shoved one's nose. The pain was terrific, my nose deformed terribly.

I was admitted to the hospital for observation and moved to a general medicine ward to wait it out. It was 8pm. I had been bleeding for 14 hours and in the hospital for 10 of those. For the moment and for the next 4 hours the blood flow was nonexistent or minimal.

Once in the room there was no peace. My senses were bombarded, noise from the nursing station, light from an open door, lingering antiseptic smells, the feel of a plastic bed liner under the sheets. Through the night my roommate, shackled to his bed, still in his lock-up jumpsuit thrashed in the throes of DTs. This would be a sleepless night that much was certain.

Then at 1AM, six hours after the transfusion and the cessation of bleeding, I felt a postnasal drip and the metallic, astringent taste of blood. Expectorating into a basin confirmed the nosebleed had started again. A quick blood test showed that my INR had been halved to 1.6, but the bleeding was not entirely stopped even though it did not rage the way it had during the day. The attending physician and I huddled. She recommended that although my INR was lower I needed to have general surgery to repair the damage and stop the bleeding once and for all.

I was difficult patient. The terror of surgery under ether I experienced as a five year old having a badly displaced broken arm set had never been fully forgotten. It was not the vivid geometric figures I observed while under its effects that were so disturbing then, but rather that I could not make the sharp-edged, multicolor zigzag lines stop moving or go away on command. As someone early in the seventh decade of their life, I was not unaware either that the risks of general anesthesia increase steadily with age.

I demurred. Finally after further consultation I agreed to the procedure, but not before sending the by now obligatory "good-bye" text to my sleeping children, a bit of self-indulgent hyperbole, I admit. So at 4AM, in an OR empty of other patients I underwent nasal surgery.

Anesthesia turned out to be much like what I envision death to be, a loss of consciousness followed by blackness, nothingness. The only difference is whether one wakes up. I did, of course, slipping in and out of consciousness for an hour in the recovery room. A void existed in my mental life. Weeks later I read the report of what happened in my absence.

––––––

Transcript of Operation

Indication for the Procedure:

This is a 64 year-old male with a history of Coumadin use for DVT, who presented to the ER yesterday morning with epistaxis (nosebleed)*. He has undergone several interventions in the ER and in the clinic including packing, correction of his coagulopathy, and cauterization with silver nitrate. Despite all these interventions, he has continued to bleed. After discussion with the patient, the decision was made to go to the operating room for nasal endoscopy and endoscopic control of epistaxis.

Description of the Procedure:

The patient was taken to the operating room and placed on the operating room table in supine position. General endotracheal anesthesia via rapid sequence induction without complication. The patient was draped in usual sterile fashion. The nasal cavities were examined with a 0 degree endoscope. Attention was first turned to the left nasal cavity. The packing was removed from the nose and copious clot was suctioned from the nasal cavity, and the nasal cavity was irrigated. The mucosa of the left nasal cavity was very traumatized and denuded in several areas from repeated packing and intervention. Afrin pledgets (pads soaked in a decongestant that works by constricting blood vessels) were then placed into the nose and attention was turned to the right nasal cavity. Again, the packing was removed. All the clots were suctioned and the nose was irrigated. The right side of the nose appeared relatively healthy with the exception of some bleeding on the right anterior septum. Afrin-soaked pledgets again were placed on the right side of the nose. Attention was turned back to the left side of the nose.

Examination of the nasal cavity revealed clot and bleeding from an apparent branch of the left sphenopalatine (a nasal artery) in the area of the posterior attachment of the middle turbinate (the sinus below the eye). This area was cauterized until there was no further bleeding noticed. The remainder of the left nasal cavity did not appear to have any brisk bleeding. A couple of small bleeders were touched with the suction cautery, but care was taken not to cauterize too much within left nasal cavity given the extensive denuded mucosa. Attention was then turned to the right nasal cavity. The area of the right septum that was bleeding was controlled. Care was taken not to cauterize extensively and there was no further bleeding. No cauterization was performed on the left anterior septum to avoid perforation (to avoid burning a hole from the left nostril through the septum into the right nostril). The nose was then filled with FloSeal thrombin (a clotting agent). An OG tube was passed. The contents of the stomach were evacuated (The stomach was pumped to remove large quantities of swallowed blood). That patient was then turned back to anesthesia where he was extubated and transferred to the PACU in stable condition.

* Parenthetical comments are author added.

———

All I cared at the time was that the bleeding had stopped. I was returned to my room where my co-occupant apparently had survived the hallucinating effects of the DTs only to be awakened to a nurse's temperance lecture that was in full throat when I arrived. Her descriptions of premature death from alcohol poisoning seemed to have little impact. I suspected he was well aware of the consequences of his behavior. The familiarity of the nurse with the patient suggested also that he was a regular who had heard the sermon before. Later in the day with no evidence of further bleeding I was discharged saluting my fellow internee on the way out.

Therapeutic Dilemmas

Following surgery, I was in a depleted state. The blood loss had been substantial. On every major hemametric measure I was below the levels expected of a healthy individual. This was particularly true of indicators of the oxygen carrying capacity of blood. The red blood cell count was low as was hematocrit, the percentage of the blood made up of red blood cells and most significantly hemoglobin, the oxygen carrying pigment that gives red blood cells their color. In a nutshell I had traumatic anemia with very rapid onset.

The condition was manifest as soon as I was ambulatory. The day after surgery I took a short walk only to find that just minor exertion left me breathless. Walking the slightest incline brought on vigorous panting while negotiating a one-flight set of stairs without stopping midway to catch my breath was out of the question. Of course, these were symptoms of a PE as well as anemia, but with a proximate cause fresh in mind, I never entertained an alternative explanation. But then neither did the ENT specialist who recommended I embark on an iron-rich diet. So I began a not unpleasant postoperative therapeutic regimen of gorging on red meat and hamburgers.

Also misleading was the reoccurrence of nosebleeds on three occasions in the week following the operation. The first prompted me leave a theater in haste followed by a frantic dash again by cab to the same emergency room. A quick blood test confirmed my INR was 1.0. Any residual anticoagulation effect from the presurgical Coumadin treatment was nonexistent thanks to the transfusion. After an hour of caring for myself in the holding area I found I could once again stop a nosebleed the old fashioned way, with packing and pressure. I checked myself out of the ER satisfied that I could deal with any future exigency.

The persistence of the bleeding was more worrisome for the ENT specialist however. I was the most difficult case he had ever encountered he claimed. He admonished me not to exercise strenuously or to lift any more than five pounds. To prevent further bleeding he asked me to refrain from restarting a Coumadin regimen until the nostrils had time to heal fully. At first he asked that I wait a week. As the number of repeat bleeds mounted he extended the time to a full month.

Conversely, my primary care physician advocated a return to an anticoagulation regimen immediately after surgery. Banking on the fact that daily doses of Coumadin would take nearly a week to reach a therapeutic level and even longer to present an appreciable bleeding risk, he reasoned that the surgery site would heal sufficiently in the meantime.

As the patient, I was caught in the middle, presented with an insoluble dilemma of conflicting recommendations and competing therapeutic options. There were real risks on both sides, each with the potential to precipitate grave consequences, perhaps life threatening ones. The therapies were diametrically opposed in action and consequence. How then could I avoid the Scylla of too little anticoagulation and potential clotting on the one hand and the Charybdis of too much anticoagulation and the possibility of excessive bleeding on the other? How would it be possible to navigate the risks without being swallowed by the maelstrom of iatrogenic therapies in competition?

The most frustrating aspect of the decision was a lack of absolutes. Neither decision was demonstrably better than the other. Both physicians were correct in their recommendations and both could be proven terribly wrong. Both had my best interests and good health at heart. While the risks of avoiding either therapy could be calculated individually no calculus existed to evaluate risk versus reward when considering the contradictory options in tandem. There was simply no way to equate the two risks simultaneously in order to choose the lesser of two evils.

One vexing aspect of the situation was there was no overarching medical authority I could turn to help make the decision, a person to break the tie. Someone I could put my faith in, whose orders I could follow with confidence. I needed a disinterested medical arbiter who by virtue of experience-granted wisdom, judgment or acumen could help me evaluate the risks. At an elemental level, I wanted an advocate who, if nothing else, could prevent me from making a horrible and preventable mistake.

But more than that, I wanted it to be someone who could appreciate how I viewed the situation and how I weighed the options. I wanted to be, in fact needed to be, part of this evaluation in order to offer my views on what was important to me, which came down to, simply enough, which risk I feared most. I was more than willing to make the final decision of which course to pursue, I simply wanted an empathetic and trusted resource to consider my nonmedical concerns and ultimately help me assess the risks though the lens of my ego-centered focus.

Not knowing what to do, with no signposts to point the way, I called on a friend, Irv Feferman, an ER specialist and trusted resource. Irv was no more definitive than the other physicians about what I should do but he performed a near priceless function nonetheless. He was a sympathetic sounding board off of whom I could reflect not only the facts of my condition, but my needs, situational exigencies as well as fears. I could count on him to respond with calm judgment earned over a career of dealing with crises. Irv did not make decisions for me but with his counsel I felt more competent to make them for myself.

Feeling more confident and not alone, I grasped the nettle and tried to make the decision on rational grounds. The typical rehabilitative period for a person having a DVTs and PEs is six months on a therapeutic regimen of Coumadin, I reasoned. I reached that mark on the day of my nosebleed. Although it was recommended that I stay on Coumadin for a full year because the PE was idiopathic or "unprovoked" in medical parlance this was just an added precaution.

Moreover, I was demonstrably better. All the signs of incipient disease were gone. My health had been restored so the nosebleed specifically and excessive bleeding generally appeared to represent the greater threat. The traumatic memories of choking on my own blood were very fresh. The desperation of not being able to breathe was not. I opted to follow the advice of the ENT specialist and stopped taking Coumadin while my nose healed.

Almost immediately I regretted the decision. If it is possible to feel DVTs form I could. Every day I sensed pain following the path of my veins from the lower leg, behind my knee, up into my thigh and finally my groin. The superficial veins were palpable and became solid to the touch. It was as if I could trace the progression of the disease up my leg tracking the path of pain and hardening vessels. This did not bode well for what was happening at a deeper level. My fear and anxiety rose concomitantly, day-by-day. Little did I know it was already too late.

The suspected anemia meanwhile seemed to improve albeit grudgingly and I continued to attribute breathlessness on exertion to it. But slow improvement and growing anxiety about what if anything was happening in my leg began to germinate seeds of doubt. What if I were not anemic? What if I already had had another PE after all and was just recovering from it?

The implications of this fretful line of thought left me with a hollow feeling. I could very well be the architect of my own ill health or in the worst case my own demise. Why was I so obstinate about making my own decisions? Second-guessing of this sort rekindled old feelings of anger, guilt and self-loathing. I mentally replayed the events and decisions that lead to this point hoping to find substantiation for my choice and absolve myself of culpability.

Irv in particular was quick to voice alarm when I described the persistent symptoms to him. In his mind there was no longer any doubt as to which risk was more imminent and threatening. He advised me to return immediately to the ER and have a diagnostic CT scan of my lungs performed to see if I had had another PE. With my history, he stressed, it was the only prudent course of action. I wish it had been that simple.

I was away from home. I had no known local medical resources to fall back on. No medical relationships, built up over years of interaction, I could count on to have a shared familiarity with my history. If indeed I had a PE my care would have to be provided by a hospital and its emergency room, by an assigned medical team with unknown expertise, in addition to necessitating an extended stay in unfamiliar surroundings.

· But the trip home required a long plane ride that had its own risks. If I had indeed had another PE the pressurized cabin could be a problematic environment. Worse yet, were I to have a PE in route there was little chance of landing and getting emergency care in time to affect the outcome. No one needed to remind me of how that would play out, waiting helpless for a verdict of life or death. No matter how slim the odds of a reoccurrence my gut feel told me it was not wise to keep doubling down, staking my existence on continuing to win life's lottery.

So I reverted to form, repeating old behaviors in order to avoid making a decision. I cherry picked the events of the past week selecting only those facts that would confirm the belief that I was anemic. A postoperative ultrasound was negative. The leg was clear of DVDs. Physical challenges came next. Running up stairs, as an example, to prove to myself that the breathlessness was transient and improving from day-to-day. Listening to me debate the options again, an increasingly exasperated Irv finally said "I can't understand why you haven't gone for a CT scan yet? With your history you should not delay."

This was unwelcome news since the flight was the next morning. It was already evening, little time remained to alter my plans. I began to fret and second-guess the decision to return home. I called the group practice of my primary care physician in Florida to get a second opinion on the advisability of traveling home and got the doctor on call, a person unfamiliar to me. The Internist agreed with Irv when he heard my history and symptoms. He recommended in no uncertain terms that I go immediately to the ER for a CT scan. It was unwise to wait, he cautioned and foolhardy to fly.

The unequivocal admonition brought back long buried feelings about the original crisis and its aftermath. Unlike the first occasion, this time I would know precisely what was happening if another vascular accident occurred. Sudden death would be the preoccupation this time not the event itself. I would have to wait helplessly for the reading of the verdict as the plane flew on with the stark knowledge of what was happening and what my chances were.

Sudden death was a fate I had avoided once through no action of my own. Since then I had recovered and had started to look forward to a long life. As time passed, I was able to convince myself the PE had been a onetime case of colossal bad luck. Part of the recovery process had been to repress the preoccupation with death and the ever present expectation of dread of the dark, being alone with my thoughts. To think now that I would be reimmersed in that kind of moment focused life and apocalyptic thinking made my stomach drop, as if hitting a bottomless air pocket in flight.

By this time though, I had made the decision to return to Florida, where I could have the confirmatory tests and treatment if need be in familiar surroundings. Although I too was virtually certain by this point that I had experienced another PE, I still hoped that I would be proven wrong. I had already made the arrangements, homecoming appointments with a vascular specialist to have another ultrasound, an ENT specialist to evaluate my post-surgical recovery, the Pulmonologist to determine the need for a CT scan, and my Internist to discuss the continuation of Coumadin therapy. It would be a whirlwind, but definitive tour of my health status. I decided to chance it.

While I may not be good at making decisions, carrying through with them once made usually is not a problem. The next morning I boarded the plane and headed to Florida. I came prepared, an oxy-meter to monitor the oxygen saturation in my blood, hemostatic tape to stop a nose bleed if need be and a syringe of Lovenox in case of emergency. After all the angst of the weeks before, the three hour flight was downright pleasant. Pleasant that is, if one doesn't count checking the time every two to three minutes to see how much flight time remained.

The day after arriving home, two weeks post-surgery, I obtained another ultrasound of my leg veins to determine if my suspicions new DVTs were present was justified. It revealed evidence of ancient clots that had calcified and were firmly attached to the vein wall. No risk of them breaking off and creating another PE. The remaining veins appeared clear with the single exception of what might be a nascent clot forming behind my knee. It was a mixed bag, not unequivocally negative for new DVTs but it did seem to support the negative findings of the ultrasound performed three days after surgery in New York. Or so I thought at the time.

Discussing the findings with the vascular specialist did not give me a sense that there was anything to worry about, nothing that demanded immediate intervention. I could give myself Lovenox shots through the weekend, he suggested, to temporarily restore anticoagulation if I wanted extra protection. But, as before, this would increase the possibility that another uncontrollable bleed would start. Putting faith in what I believed were the positive ultrasound findings I decided to forego the weekend Lovenox shots, a fateful decision as it turned out.

Monday I had a day of doctor appointments scheduled intended to determine if I needed a CT scan to rule out another embolism. I rose, walked to the bathroom and made it only half way to the shower. Just as before, I took one step spanning the chasm from healthy to sick. I could not breathe – again. I staggered back to the bed panting. It was another PE I was sure, but this attack did not seem as severe as the original. While my wife dialed 911, I began to dissemble and deny.

When the ambulance arrived I debated whether it should go to the hospital or to the doctor appointments as planned. Finally, an EMT took charge. Summarizing the obvious he said, "You are cold and clammy. Your pulse is racing. The oxygen saturation in your blood is 87%. It's hospital time". I agreed to be transported to the ER in the ambulance, proving it is possible to learn from experience, but only after insisting I walk to the waiting vehicle, proving one can never stop enjoying the benefits of more education.

On the way I was fitted for an oxygen mask. An IV was inserted. Ten minutes later I was delivered to the ER door this time by-passing reception, billing and triage. The obligatory CT scan was ordered and the results confirmed another PE.

———

Examination: CTA Chest

Clinical History:

Shortness of Breath

Results:

There are extensive filling defects (clots) in the right main pulmonary artery as well as extending towards the peripheral branches in all directions.

There is a similar clot in the lower left lobe and left upper lobe pulmonary artery branches.

Impression:

Extensive bilateral pulmonary emboli

———

While this PE was not as immediately life threatening as the first, it was much more extensive involving both lungs and leaving just one of six lobes unaffected. A Lovenox shot was administered and I was admitted to the hospital. So began a nine-day stay in the hospital while I waited for the Coumadin dosage to be calibrated and my INR to reach therapeutic levels again. This was a process with which I was by now completely familiar.

I was given another ultrasound, my third in two weeks. To my complete surprise, the leg that was seemingly clear on Friday had multiple DVTs on Monday. The possibility that DVTs could form so rapidly simply defied logic. The findings were incomprehensible and left me shaking my head in disbelief. The explanation for the discrepancy would not emerge for another three months.

Pondering Imponderables

The hospital stay was interminable. A period of suspended animation during which I waited and watched as my INR inched up in painfully small increments toward the therapeutic threshold of 2.0, the hurdle that had to be cleared before I would be granted freedom. I filled the hours of ennui puzzling over several enduring mysteries that remained after the preceding weeks.

What caused the nosebleed? I have no way to be sure but I can hypothesize a plausible sequence of events. The New York apartment uses a forced hot air system that creates an arid environment. After a week or two in desert like conditions the membranes in my nostrils dried out and were susceptible to small, innocuous and otherwise eminently controllable nosebleeds. Controllable, that is, without Coumadin in the mix.

The progress of the bleeding is consistent with the way Coumadin works. It blocks the reuptake of Vitamin K after first use making it less available to ignite the coagulation cascade as time goes on. That explains why the first nosebleed was insignificant and easily stopped whereas bleeding became an unstoppable deluge after the initial effect of Vitamin K was spent and subsequently delayed. The medical interventions, while well meaning, did little other than add new bleeding sites and aggravated existing ones.

In the final analysis the episode was a case of a minor injury spiraling rapidly out of control due to a confluence of aleatory circumstances and actions. Shit happens, in other words, as a result of mindless, unfeeling, undirected chance. Life is a game of chance with a certain outcome eventually.

Was it anemia from blood loss of a PE? Again I will never know for certain. But with the luxury of dispassion from my back casting gaze I think it is probable that when the transfusion crashed my anticoagulation and my INR plummeted to 1.6, halved in a matter of a few hours, I enter a hyper-coagulated state, making clotting more likely not only in my nose but throughout my body. It is entirely likely, in my opinion, that I had a series of small PEs in the weeks following surgery and the first occurred while I was on the operating table. The change, from excellent respiration before surgery to breathlessness after, was just too extreme to be otherwise.

How could DVTs develop so quickly? This question bewildered me the most. How could I be free of DVTs on a Friday afternoon and yet have at least one develop over the weekend to the point it could cause a PE on Monday morning. I was at a loss to explain it. I asked every nurse, technician and doctor I came in contact with to explain how it was possible. I never got a satisfactory answer.

That is, until I had a progress ultrasound several months after leaving the hospital. The same technician who had done the first ultrasound on the Friday preceding the PE event administered it. He is a man whose skill I admire and whose knowledge of his craft and the underlying physiology of venous disease I respect. I posed the same question to him as I lay on the examining table. How could I be DVT free just two days before the PE?

"Oh but you weren't", he said. "Your leg was filled with DVTs. It's right here in my report." He read me the pertinent sections as I listened with mouth agape.

I had seen the vascular specialist immediately after the Friday ultrasound and other than mentioning the ancient and inert clots from the seven months earlier and the nascent clot behind my knee he did not indicate any DVTs that I recall. I left the office with no sense that there was anything amiss, nothing that required immediate attention and could not wait until I had seen the Pulmonologist on Monday. No treatment was suggested or recommended. Rather it was left as my prerogative to take Lovenox or not over the weekend.

He may have not communicated the seriousness of the situation or felt it was not serious at all. Or I might have missed his meaning in the professional relativism of his assessment. How such a complete and portentous breakdown in communication occurred remains for me the biggest mystery of the whole affair.

CHAPTER EIGHT
EPILOGUE—STARTING OVER

"Live as if you were to die tomorrow. Learn as if you were to live forever."

—*Mahatma Gandhi*
(1869 – 1948)

My life is a work in progress.

The series of PE's precipitated by the near fatal bleeding event set me back six months. I found myself in the same hospital struggling for breath just as before. It was as if the second PE reset the clock erasing all the recovery I had made, simply eliminating any progress accomplished over the intervening time. And yet, as time went on I began to notice lasting changes that had occurred as a by-product of the first attack and recovery from it.

As foreshadowed by the difficulty and extended time it took for the Coumadin regimen to bring my INR back to therapeutic levels, twice as long and the need for stronger doses to do so, the physical recovery from the second event was much more protracted than the first. With the first instance physical recovery was progressive, linear, and rapid. I could feel and the physiological metrics would periodically confirm that I was making steady, almost daily, progress toward my pre-attack state. After six months just as the bleeding and next PE events were about to happen, I had for all intents and purposes returned to full pre-embolism health. Now I was back at the starting line. It was discouraging to say the least.

On top of this the recovery process was not nearly as dramatic or demonstrated such uniform improvement. At times there would be spurts of improvement, followed by a plateau and a lengthy hiatus before moving ahead again. On a few occasions I regressed. Symptoms that disappeared one month would be back a month or two later only to disappear again eventually. It took a full year to make it all the way back from the second PE. Nevertheless, although the healing process was tedious and often frustrating, it did not send me into a boundless pit of depression as it had before.

The damage was of a different character as well. Whereas the first clot was massive and effectively stopped my right lung from functioning, once the clot began to break up and blood flow was restored to the lung, my breathing recovered very quickly. The second PE was as massive the first but more extensive, affecting 85% of my lung function, and less concentrated. It was less acute or immediately life threatening as a result.

The biggest difference was when the second PE started to break up the clots moved down in the pulmonary arteries in the process putting pressure on the lining of the lungs, the pleurisy. While lungs have no sensory nerves the pleurisy does. So although the lungs did not register the presence of the PE in the form of pain, when the pleurisy became involved the pain was excruciating. For a two month period in the aftermath of the PE I experienced constant and significant pain across my back and chest until the clots dissolved to the point that they were no longer in contact with the lung lining. This was a new and unpleasant side effect I had not encountered after the first PE but unlike if it had happened before, I took it in stride.

What differed most though between the first and second recovery was my reaction to the precipitating event, the illness and my recovery from it. Looking back with the benefit of having two events to compare, I understood that I had a nasty case of PTSD the first go round. The second time I had very few PTSD symptoms. The night terrors, violent or symbolic dreams did not recur. I did not rage at the unfairness of my circumstance, feel the need to blame anyone, except perhaps myself, or fantasize about malpractice. Other signs and symptoms of PTSD such as moods swings, deep depression, cognitive impairment, withdrawal and emotional numbing were not in evidence or greatly attenuated. I had put all that away.

Many of the same physical complications recurred, yet did not illicit the same response. There were instances of shooting pain in my leg for no apparent reason as an example. For months, my leg would swell at night or after sitting for a long time just as before. But these sequeale did not incite fear or bring me to the point of panic and dread. I was not nearly as watchful. It takes an enormous amount of energy to sustain the vigilance that accompanies PTSD. To my great relief, as if exhaling from a long held breath, I did not seem to have the need to watch myself so closely the second time. Perhaps the greatest relief of my second convalescence was the realization that – yes PTSD is a real disease, debilitating and paralyzing at times, but in the end it is transitory. A person can and does recover from it. I did.

Much of the reason for the absence of PTSD symptoms may have been due to the "work" I had done in the months after the first PE. I was mentally prepared with an experiential knowledge of what was to come and I was not as emotionally vulnerable as a result. Sudden death remained a possibility but I did not try to deny or repress the thought. I did not dwell on it or react in the same way when I acknowledged the possibility.

I recall quite vividly when I noticed the change, while I was swimming. My leg is often in pain and cramped over the course of a long swim. Previously these symptoms of exertion would prompt morbid concern and anxiety to the point that if it were the least bit unusual I would stop the laps prematurely, sometimes mid-lane. As was my superstitious wont I always kept a Lovenox injector poolside just in case.

On the day of insight the pain was present as usual as I was swimming. As I watched the blue lane line below me glide by I thought: I could die suddenly if the exertion and kicking loosed another embolism. I acknowledged the possibility to myself; yes – I could die; yes – little could be done to save me if it happened; yes – I would never be able to say goodbye to my family, to tell them one last time that I loved them or live to watch their lives unfold; yes – I would cease to exist for all that implied. I acknowledged all this, accepted the validity of it and kept swimming.

My relationship with the medical profession had changed dramatically overtime and mostly for the better. Clearly much of the early conflict with the caregivers and the care I received was a direct result of PTSD. I was angry at being a victim of what I deemed to be inadequate care that could have otherwise prevented the original PE. I carried an outsized chip on my shoulder and a sense of entitlement that would not quit.

But I worked through all those feeling overtime. I understood how debilitating and unhealthy those ideations were and how they retarded my recovery. Only when I learned to forgive my caregivers for their contribution and recognize my own did I move beyond the need to find a villain and seek retribution. It was perhaps the most positive thing I did during the recovery. I only wish my physician and I had been able to discuss the causes of the first embolism in a nonthreatening or accusatory fashion in a safe environment. It leaves a hole in our relationship that we did not.

There are other aspects involving the structure and delivery of medical care that if changed would have improved my recovery I believe. I wonder about the wisdom of the Hospitalist position, not the utility, the wisdom. Whether it is wise to introduce a new professional into the mix at a critical juncture when the patient is in most need of familiarity, continuity and trust. I would have liked my primary physician to have done hospital rounds at least once during my stay instead of being inaccessible behind walls of physicians, nurses and liaisons.

I wonder too why counseling after a near death event is not routinely offered or why patients who have just had a traumatic medical event are not routinely screened for PTSD. The majority will not have it but getting professional counseling for the minority who do would improve after-emergency care immeasurably and if my behavior is any model may help prevent conflict between patients and doctors.

Finally, I see a need for an overall management function in the delivery of care, a physician who manages a patient's health profile but does not necessarily treat or act as just a referral agent to a host of specialists. Primary care physicians are supposed to play this role but I found them to be more concierge than manager.

In the weeks leading up to the second PE, I learned important lessons about myself. Chief among these was that although I grew up in a medical family and had been involved in medical research in one form or another all my career I was not a physician. I knew just enough to be a great danger to myself by wanting to control every situation, to make every decision and thinking I was knowledgeable enough to do so. But in the end, I found that trust and faith in my physician mattered more than control. While it is still important I believe for the patient to have ultimate authority over their treatment, it should be exercised by veto dictated by emotion not by information. I am still a strong believer in the ability of the patient to feel the right decision, not as what to do but what not to do.

My religious grazing lead to no new satisfying end point, I am disappointed to say. After all that had happened I was no more able than before to find hope, solace or the promise of salvation in any of the faith-based religions. I remained agnostic, persuadable only by evidence and an empiricist to the end. Reincarnation is not a testable premise or more precisely testable while we live, because we cannot recall previous temporal manifestations of our immortal consciousness. If we cannot, it does not matter whether the hypothesis is true or not since it does not affect our lives or improve our existential condition. In the final analysis I classified reincarnation with other faith-founded religious beliefs I rejected.

I am comfortable with the notion that chance is the driving force in our lives. No grand architect is required to explain origin of the universe. No omniscient or omnipotent entity needs to exist to explain what happens in our lives. No god can be expected to answer a spiritual mayday and intervene in our lives to change them on our behalf and to our benefit. Prayer may calm us but it does nothing to change the odds. I can accept the arbitrary, unfeeling and godlessness of chance. Even so, still doubting, still seeking, I often wonder about the stranger on the beach and the question he put to me.

Buddhism, minus reincarnation, was the closest I came to finding a belief system with which I had some degree of affinity, one that could help me deal with my own mortality. I could appreciate the basic humanism of its teachings. It seemed to me that Buddhism focused on the crucial existential issues – impermanence, suffering, death – confronted in the here and now not in a place and manner that happens outside our experience only after death. And who could argue with the goal of eliminating suffering.

Well I could actually. Our obsessive attachment to ever changing and impermanent things and relationships might very well be the source of all suffering but detachment in order to lessen suffering seemed to me to be a self-defeating means of ending it. If suffering were the price for loving and living I would gladly pay it. Suffering is poignantly delicious, bitter and sweet, not in a masochistic way but rather because it signifies that I am alive. I have taken the chance to live and love and enjoyed it all to the fullest. Detachment from life is practicing for death by playing dead. I cherish my suffering. When I die I want to suffer mightily at the end of my existence, to mourn a life that was filled with living. One I loved in all its aspects, good and bad, and loved perhaps too dearly.

The second PE gave me what proved to be a fortuitous opportunity to have a second chance to change things that I was not able to get right after the first. It was a Mulligan to correct errant motivational drives that had not gone in the right direction, to refocus and take a second swing. This was most apparent in my professional life. During the first recovery period I had attempted to change my orientation to work. I realized I would need to reduce my commitments if I were to redirect my life toward activities that were truly meaningful for me. But I was engaged in so many business ventures it was difficult to disengage. I wanted to complete each of them and then I would be ready to start anew.

Despite my best efforts in this regard, the goal proved illusory. Resolutions to problems were never on my expedited schedule, business partners did not have the same sense of urgency and often had different objectives. So over time I got progressively more deeply engaged trying to bend decisions to my point of view and timeline. By the time of the second embolism I was just as engaged, aggressive and tense as I was before I had the first medical emergency.

While in the hospital recuperating after another near fatal PE, I was about to pick-up again where I had left off. I read monthly board reports, compared views with fellow board members, and tried to weigh in on the issues of the day. Fortunately a well-timed avuncular conversation with a good friend and sometime business partner made me realize how little I had changed and how out of control I still was. He gently admonished me for not concentrating on what was really important – my health. Instead he pointed out I continued to tempt fate while in pursuit of comparatively trivial and meaningless objectives, ones I wanted to shed in fact.

It is hard to come to the realization that one is expendable, that decisions made without you will not necessarily be worse or even better. They will just be different. Letting go and moving on is not the same as finishing up I realized. I accepted this and started to let go understanding that matters would play out over a course that I would not determine and should not second guess. This was the most difficult reorientation of all for me especially given how many psychological and financial threads were tied together in it, the need to be productive, to have something to say worth heeding, to be vital and in my case to be proven right. It remains a struggle to stay uninvolved. I find I must make a concerted effort not to second guess others, to forget the old slights and betrayals and to avoid the temptation to jump back in. I still struggle with my need to control and to always be proven right. I probably always will.

Taking a Mulligan on life extended to my personal relationships as well. In the aftermath of both PE's I wanted nothing more than to withdraw from the social world and to put my familial interactions on hold. It was a necessary and self-protective impulse given what I was dealing with. I especially wanted to avoid relationships that contributed to my illness, tinged with negative connotations, conflict, competitiveness, animosity and incivility to name a few. Additionally ones that were just not satisfying because I shared too few interests with the other person. But I realized after the second PE that my self-imposed isolation had served its purpose. The emotions that were dulled by PTSD were awakened once more. As I felt better and my stamina returned I wanted to re-engage the social world, to rekindle old friendships that I had let lapse and repair ones that had ended badly.

Today my recovery is such that at last I have been cleared to scuba dive again and to work my way up to high altitude trekking. But I don't feel compelled to cram my life full of as many trips as possible or to wring every ounce of achievement out of each one. My goals are more circumspect but just as satisfying and much more liberating. Accomplishments can be more limited now – less likely to demand completion of extreme feats or to attain lofty ends. While I still hope to travel to Mt. Kailash someday and would dearly love to circumnavigate it perhaps that is just not in the cards. I can accept that now. I can stand at the foot of the mountain and watch the pilgrims without having to be one.

This does not mean that my life today is totally serene or complete or ever will be. I still get depressed on occasion but I have the newly found patience to wait knowing the lethargy, ennui and feelings of hopelessness will pass. I worry that I am being left behind because of my illnesses, marginalized and diminished but I have confidence the path I have chosen is right for me. I am not totally sure I have settled on what the most meaningful activities are for me going forward. Perhaps I will never know. What I have done is minimize the ones that give me neither enjoyment nor inner peace.

Relationships can be stormy at times despite the strength of their foundation. And mostly I have yet to remove the highest barrier to ego integration – the ability to forgive myself and love the person I am despite my myriad shortcomings. I do not know if the journey to self-understanding and acceptance ever ends. But I do know that without a series of sudden life events I would never have fully understood the need to take the first step.

It gives me great joy then to accept that my life remains a work in progress.

NOTES

Chapter One: A Survivor's Tale

What is a Massive Pulmonary Embolism?

Pulmonary emboli are typically categorized into three types depending on severity: 1. Massive, 2. Non-massive, and 3. Low-risk. Approximately 5% of PE's are massive, 40% are non-massive and the remaining 55% are low-risk, essentially sub-acute to the point on non-recognition.

The clinical definition of the first of these – a massive pulmonary embolism, the sort I had, is having "sustained hypotension (systolic blood pressure <90 mm) for at least 15 minutes". In laymen's terms this means the blood clot, when it settles in the lungs, impedes blood flow to the degree that it is inadequately pumped throughout the rest of the body. The victim's blood pressure falls in response. The bigger the clot, the greater the restriction, the lower the blood pressure.

The physical symptoms associated with hypotension are the ones I experienced on the beach, feeling cold, clammy and sweating. No one was on the beach to measure my blood pressure for 15 minutes, of course, to see if it met the definitional standard. I am basing my assertion that I had a massive PE based on the severity and duration of the physical symptoms I experienced and the assessment of the Pulmonologist after the fact.

The best estimate I could find of death from a massive PE is provided by the International Cooperative Pulmonary Embolism Registry (ICOPER), a study of 2,454 patients in 52 hospitals in 7 countries in North America and Europe. For a massive PE death occurs within 90 days in the range of 43% to 62% of the cases with the best estimate being 52% of the time. Most of the deaths occur in one to two hours after the attack. I based my estimate that the odds of my dying on the beach again on the severity of the symptoms and from the comments of my Pulmonologist. So I used the top end of the range.

The clinical definition for a massive and non-massive PE's can be found in AHA (American Heart Association) Scientific Statement. Management of Massive and Submassive Pulmonary Embolism, Idiofemoral Deep Vein Thrombosis, and Clinical Thrombolitic Pulmonary Hypertension. <u>Circulation</u> 123: 1788 –1830, 2011.

A good summary of the categorization and distribution of PE events is given in Kucher, N. et al. *Massive Pulmonary Embolism*. <u>Circulation</u> 113: 577 – 82, 2006.

Lovenox

Lovenox is the trade name for Enoxaparin a powerful, fast acting low molecular weight heparin anticoagulant that is derived from pig intestines. Its principal value for a person who has had a PE and is at risk for more thromboses or emboli is to provide almost instantaneous anticoagulation. Immediately upon injection Lovenox greatly inhibits the body's ability to form clots thereby reducing the likelihood the patient will have another DVT or PE which in my case probably would have been fatal. Sustained use also provides therapeutic benefit helping the clot to dissolve.

Other anticoagulants, especially the standard therapies warfarin and its trade equivalent Coumadin, take an extended period of time to build up in the blood stream to the point they provide reliable prophylactic and therapeutic anticoagulation. For example, it took 4 days before I became "therapeutic" on warfarin after my first PE and nine days after the second PE. The patient is at risk throughout this ramp up period so Lovenox is used as a bridge therapy, providing the needed therapeutic anticoagulation until warfarin has reached an acceptable level.

As a drug, Lovenox has very few side effects and is easy to use. The liquid is injected in the fat surrounding the midriff. The down sides are the beneficial effect has a short half-life, 12 hours, so two shots per day are required and the cost, $100/shot. The other unique after side effect of using the product is that because it causes instant anticoagulation there is considerable bleeding at the site of the injection. This leads to some spectacular bruising around one's lower abdomen after a few days of use.

Ellen's Version

There are a few factual discrepancies between my recall of the events of March 21st 2012 when the first PE occurred. My sister remembers hearing my telephone call while in Bailey's General Store. My recollection is the call reached my wife and sister as they were driving home. Perhaps that was the second call. She also believes I took a ride home with them when we met on the road to our house. I recall refusing the offer to ride and walked instead.

Given the well-known fact that memories of the same event can vary significantly between people I find the factual differences between my account and that of my sister to be very minor. I have left each account as the author remembered it therefore.

Chapter Two: Hospitalization

The Epidemiology of Pulmonary Embolism

Epidemiology is the study of the causes and distribution of disease within populations and communities. Of principal concern of epidemiologists are basic metrics of disease: incidence – the number of cases that occur in the population in a year (often expressed as a rate per some unit of population, e.g., 100,000 people or exposure e.g., number per person years), morbidity – the number or persons who currently have the disease again expressed in raw numbers or rates, and mortality – the number of people who die from the disease within the year. The basic statistics are then arrayed against other variables such as age, race or gender to note significant correlations and relationships between the disease and populations subgroups.

The epidemiology of PE's, its incidence, prevalence and mortality, are extremely difficult to estimate accurately or with any degree of precision for a number of reasons. First with respect to incidence, the most serious cases are acute, life threatening and not amenable to accurate categorization or study. On the opposite extreme cases can be so minor that they are not recorded in the statistics at all. So it is difficult to come to a solid number of PE's that occur each year.

Generally, statistics gathered among hospital patients tend to be the best especially cause of death and mortality figures since autopsies are more apt done. Offsetting this is the fact that hospital patients are more likely to have classic risk factors for PE's, immobility, cancer and surgery, so there would be greater prevalence and incidence among this group. The cause of death might also be attributed to the presumed cause of the PE as opposed to the proximate cause, i.e., the PE itself. Mortality rates can vary in addition because time periods within which death occurs after the event are not always consistent: immediate, 90 day, one and five year mortality rates being typical time periods used.

Even the definition of what constitutes a case can change. Pulmonary emboli are often lumped with DVT's to form a new category of disease called Venous Thromboembolism or VTE's. This tends to double the incidence and prevalence rates because two diseases are counted instead of PE's alone, but lower the rates to mortality because DVT's are less often fatal than are PE's.

Given these caveats and others one could name, I attempted to assemble a realistic picture of the epidemiology of PE's, specifying the results when necessary by the time periods and definitions used in the study cited. The epidemiological statistics given in the text were drawn from a number of sources and are a compilation of the information contained in them, including:

Goldhaber, S. et al. *Acute Pulmonary Embolism: Clinical Outcomes in the International Cooperative Pulmonary Registry.* Lancet 353: 1389 – 1386.

> Arguably the best overview of the epidemiology
> of PE's using data from the ICOPER database.
> Limitations include the sample is hospital-based.

CDC Grand Rounds: *Preventing Hospital Associated Venous Thromboembolism.* 63: 190 -3, 2014.

The Surgeon General's Call to Action to Prevent Deep Vein Thrombosis and Pulmonary Embolism. 2008
www.surgeongeneral.gov/library/calls/index.html

> Two other excellent sources for basic
> epidemiologic information about DVT's, PE's and
> VTE's.

Centers for Disease Control and Prevention
www.cdc.gov/ncbddd/blooddisorders/documents/bbv_pnv_c
0_1159_thrombosis_r1mtr.pdf

> Estimates incidence of PE's to be between
> 300,000 to 600,000 per year with a third dying
> in the first month

Dobesh, P. *Economic Burden of Venous Thromboembolism in Hospitalized Patients.* Pharmacotherapy 29: 943 - 53, 2009.

> Estimates the hospital cost of DVT's and PE's to
> be $1.5 Billion per year with the cost of an initial
> PE hospitalization to be in the range of $9,600 to
> $16,600.

Haines, S. *Venous Thromboembolism: Pathophysiology and Clinical Presentation.* American Journal of System-Health Pharmacy. 60: S3 – 5, 2003

> Estimates there are 2 Million cases and 100,000
> deaths from PE's in the US each year.

White, R. *The Epidemiology of Venous Thromboembolism.* Circulation. 107:14 – 8, 2003

> Provides statistics on recurrence and death rates, how incidence increase exponentially with age, and that first time PE's are idiopathic (without identifiable cause).

White, R and Keenan, C. *Effects of Race and Ethnicity on Incidence of Venous Thromboembolism.* Thrombosis Research. 123: S11 – 7, 2009

> The title says it all.

Hospitalists

The term Hospitalists first appeared in an article by Wachler, R. and Goldman, L. *The Emerging Role of "Hospitalists" in the American Health Care System.* New England Journal of Medicine. 335: 514 – 7, 1999. Since then Hospital Medicine has become a separate specialty, training programs have been established and the discipline has its own professional organization, the Society of Hospital Medicine.

Among the responsibilities of Hospitalists listed by the Society of Hospital Medicine are:

1. Prompt and complete attention to all patient care needs including diagnosis, treatment and performance of medical procedures, and
2. Collaboration, communication, and coordination with all physicians and healthcare personnel caring for hospitalized patients.

Seen in this light, the Hospitalist I dealt with had no reason to believe she was doing anything other than performing her job and providing the best care possible when she called my Internist.

Warfarin History

The discovery of warfarin is a widely known and oft told story, among the best summaries as is often the case being provided by Wikipedia. One lesser known reference from which I took the quote by Karl Paul Link is <u>WARF: Fifty Years</u> edited by William R. Jordan III (www.warf.org/about-us/background/history/societal-contributions/societal-contributions.cmsx)

International Standardized Ratio (INR)

The metric used to determine anticoagulation among warfarin users is the International Standardized Ratio (INR). The time it takes to form a clot is known as prothrombin time or PT. In general, INR is the time it takes a person who is on an anticoagulant to form a clot ($PT_{subject}$) compared to the clotting time of some standard ($PT_{standard}$) expressed as a ratio or

$$INR = \left[PT_{subject})/ PT_{standard\}} \right]^{ISI}$$

In normal anticoagulation therapy the desired ratio ranges from 2 to 3. In other words it takes a person on warfarin two to three times longer to form a clot than the average person.

The simple ratio of subject to standard PT's is not precisely accurate because different test labs and countries use different control tissues as standards. These are not comparable with respect to basic clotting speed. An adjustment factor, the exponent ISI or International Sensitivity Index in the formula above, is used to equalize all control samples and make the test results comparable regardless of testing facility or control sample. ISI typically varies between 1 and 2.

Coumadin Related Bleeding Episodes

Budnitz, D. et al. *Emergency Departments Visits for Outpatient Adverse Drug Events: Demonstration of a National Surveillance System.* <u>Annals of Emergency Medicine.</u> 45: 197-206, 2005, and

Budnitz, D. et al. *Emergency Hospitalization for Adverse Drug Events Among Older Americans.* <u>New England Journal of Medicine.</u> 365: 2002 -12, 2011

Two excellent sources for statistics on adverse drug event-related emergency room visits in the US caused by warfarin.

Coumadin Prescriptions Per Year

The number of prescriptions written for Coumadin and warfarin is a matter of conjecture, some estimates running as high as 30 Million per year. What is known is that prescriptions are on the rise, probably as a result of an aging population. For instance, Wysowski, D. et al. state that there were 21 Million prescriptions for Coumadin/warfarin in 1998 a figure that grew to 31 Million by 2004 (JAMA Network. vol. 167 (13), July 9, 2007).

Chapter Three: The New Normal – PTSD and Treatment

Prevalence of PTSD

This is a difficult topic to get one's mind around. There are scores of studies on populations that are known to have elevated rates of PTSD after exposure to life threatening events, e.g., combat veterans, rape victims, etc. Usually, there are no simple single-value estimates for the rate of PTSD among these groups for a variety of reasons. Definition of "veteran" can vary between studies, such as all people who served vs. combat veterans as an example. The place where the study was done, like a VA center vs. a general mailed survey and time after exposure can affect estimates and so forth.

Nevertheless, I tried to obtain a single number to estimate a general prevalence of PTSD in each group so the discussion in the text was not lost in the minutiae of prevalence estimation methodologies. The goal was to show a basic commonality in the estimates regardless of cause. To emphasize the fact that, regardless to the nature of the exposure, a significant minority (around 10 to 15%) exposed to a life threatening event will suffer from PTSD afterward and the lifetime prevalence will be in the 20 to 30% range. If the estimate is fairly regular it suggests that there is a common aspect of this kind of exposure that affects a stable minority of people.

Below then are summary reviews of prevalence research or seminal studies of PTSD prevalence for select high risk groups from which I drew the prevalence estimates in the text.

National Comorbidity Survey www.hcp.med.harvard.edu/ncs/

> The best source of nationally representative estimates of mental illness in the US including PTSD.

Schnurr, P. *PTSD and Combat-related Psychiatric Symptoms in Older Veterans.* PTSD Research Quarterly. Volume 2, Winter, 1991
www.ptsd.va.gov/professional/newsletters/research-quarterly/V2N1.pdf

> The source for PTSD Prevalence rates among WWII and Korean veterans.

Cozza, S. *Combat Exposure and PTSD.* PTSD Research Quarterly. Volume 16, Winter, 2005

> The source for prevalence rates among Vietnam, Gulf War and Iraq/Afghanistan veteran.

Richardson, L. et al. *Prevalence Estimates of Combat-Related PTSD: A Critical Review* Australian and New Zealand Journal of Psychiatry. 44: 4 – 19, 2010
www.ncbi.nlm.nih.gov/pmc/articles/PMC2891773/#!po=8.75000

> Review of studies of PTSD among US and allied soldiers from the Vietnam, First Iraq War, Second Iraq War and Afghanistan. Large variability reported depending on exposure to combat but generally incidence estimates range

from 5 to 15% with lifetime rates in the 20 to
30% range.

Kilpatrick, D. *The Mental Health Impact of Rape.* National
Violence Against Women Prevention Research Center, Medical
University of South Carolina, Charleston, SC, Copyright 2000.
www.musc.edu/vawprevention/research/mentalimpact.shtml

The source for PTSD among rape victims.

Edmonson, D. et al. *Posttraumatic Stress Disorder Prevalence
and Risk of Recurrence in Acute Coronary Syndrome Patients: A
Meta-analytic Review.* American Heart Journal. 166: 806 - 14,
2013

A meta-analysis of 24 studies Acute Coronary
Syndrome (heart attack or unstable angina)
patients. Wide ranges of PTSD incidence rates
were observed between studies with the average
being 12%.

Kassam-Adams, N. et al. *Posttraumatic Stress Following
Pediatric Injury: Update on Diagnosis, Risk Factors, and
Interventions.* JAMA Pediatrics. 167:1158 - 65, 2013

Review found persistent PTSD symptoms among
1 of 6 (16.7%) children and their parents after a
pediatric injury.

Galea, S. et al. *The Epidemiology of Post-Traumatic Stress
Disorder after Disasters.* Epidemiology Review. 27:78 - 91, 2005
doi: 10.1093/epirev/mxi003

Excellent review of studies involving PTSD
incidence after large scale social disturbances
and natural disasters. Studies indicate incidence
rates generally falling in the 5 – 15% range, with
prevalence falling off rapidly after initial
exposure.

Neria, Y. et al. *Posttraumatic Stress Disorder Following the September 11, 2001 Terrorist Attacks: A Review of the Literature Among Highly Exposed Populations.* American Psychologist. 66: 429 – 446, 2011 doi.10.1037/a00244791

> A wide ranging review of various groups
> exposed to the World Trade Center attack,
> including victims, witnesses, first responders,
> and residents of the local area. The review found
> remarkably consistent PTSD rates among the
> groups for the most part in the 10 to 12% range.

Superstitious Behavior

Bandura, A. Social Learning Theory. Prentice-Hall, Englewood Cliffs, NJ, 1977, and

Bandura, A. Social Foundations of Thought and Action: A Social Cognitive Theory.

> Prentice-Hall, Englewood Cliffs, NJ, 1986

> > The two citations by Bandura above provide
> > descriptions of social learning theory based on
> > operant conditioning.

Skinner, B. *'Superstition' in the Pigeon.* Journal of Experimental Psychology. 38:168 - 172, 1947

> Skinner's classic study of the acquisition of
> superstitious behavior by pigeons in response to
> intermittent reinforcement.

Brain Imaging

Desbordes, G. et al. *Effects of mindful-attention and compassion meditation training on amygdala response to emotional stimuli in an ordinary, non-meditative state.* Frontiers of Human Neuroscience. 6: 292 doi: 10.3389/fnhum.2012.00292. eCollection 2012

Interesting article on the impact made using Buddhist meditation techniques, Cognitively-Based Compassion Training, on brain structures that are associated with PTSD.

Chapter Four: Victimization – Fate and Forgiveness

Techniques of Neutralization

Sykes, G. and Matza, D. *Techniques of Neutralization: A Theory of Delinquency*. American Sociological Review. 22: 664 - 70, 1957

Chapter Five: Facing Oblivion

Miracles

The statistics on the number of people killed annually in the US by lightning strikes is compiled and reported by NOAA: http://www.lightningsafety.noaa.gov/fatalities.htm

The Power of Prayer

The following articles form the basis of the discussion in the text around the efficacy of praying for patients.

Bensen, H. et al. *Study of the Therapeutic Effects of Intercessory Prayer (STEP) in Cardiac Bypass Patients: A Multicenter Randomized Trial of Uncertainty and Certainty of Receiving Intercessory Prayer*. American Heart Journal. 151: 934 – 42, 2006

Three study conditions: prayer (yes/no), and within prayer knowledge of being prayed for (yes/no). 604 subjects. No evidence prayer helped but knowledge of being prayed for may have hurt outcomes.

Byrd, R. *Positive Therapeutic Effects of Intercessory Prayer in a Coronary Care Unit Populations.* Southern Medical Journal. 81: 826 – 9, 1988

> 493 coronary patients assigned randomly to prayer or no prayer groups. Some positive outcomes were noted in the prayer group when compared with controls.

Harris, W. et al. *A Randomized, Controlled Trial of the Effects of Remote, intercessory Prayer on Outcomes in Patients Admitted to the Coronary Care Unit.* Archives of Internal Medicine. 159: 2273 – 8, 1999

> 990 patients assigned at random to a remote intercessory prayer group and a no prayer control. Higher scores on some measures were noted for the prayer group.

Roberts, L. et al. *Intercessory Prayer for the Alleviation of Ill Health.* Cochrane Database Systematic Reviews. 15: CD000368, 2009.

> The best and most comprehensive evidence to date. A meta-analysis of ten studies involving 7,646 patients. Found variability in the findings of the studies, several reporting positive effects for prayer but overall there was no effect for intercessory prayer.

Death and Immortality

Crick, F. The Astonishing Hypothesis: The Scientific Search for the Soul. Charles Scribner and Sons, New York, 1993

> A biological approach for the explanation of consciousness

Mitchell, S. <u>Bhagavad Gita: A New Translation.</u> Three Rivers Press, New York, 2010

> The poetic saga of the origins of reincarnation beliefs

Lickerman, A. Overcoming the Fear of Death, Blog Post March 15, 2009 www.happinessinthisworld.com

> Dr. Lickerman is one of the best voices on dealing with PTSD and fear of death and nonexistence following a near fatal event. One with whom I share a great affinity because of the closeness of our spiritual beliefs and common near death medical etiology.

Near Death Events (NDE's)

Kübler-Ross, E. <u>The Tunnel and the Light: Essential Insights on Living and Dying.</u> Marlowe and Company, New York, 1979

> Dr. Kübler-Ross' summary of her investigation into Near Death Experiences based on over 20,000 cases from her clinical practice. Later printings include A Letter to A Child with Cancer, Dr. Kübler-Ross' letter to a dying child also known as the Dougy Letter.

Alexander, E. <u>Proof of Heaven: A Neurosurgeon's Journey into the Afterlife.</u> Simon and Schuster Paperbacks, New York, 2012

> The mega bestseller describing Dr. Alexander's Near Death Experience and perhaps most memorable for the author's authority as a neurosurgeon and his systematic and erudite attempts to rule out medical and physical reasons for his experience thereby proving heaven exists.

Greyson, B. *The Near-Death Experience Scale: Construction, Reliability, and Validity.* Journal of Nervous and Mental Disease. 171:369 – 75, 1983

> Description of the "Gold Standard" scale for determining if a person has had a NDE.

Lai, C. et al. *Impact of near-death experiences on dialysis patients: a multicenter collaborative study.* Journal of Kidney Disease. 50:124 - 32, 2007

> Suggests more religious patients were more likely to have an NDE

Belanti J. et al. *Phenomenology of near-death experiences: a cross-cultural perspective.* Transcultural Psychiatry. 45:121 - 33, 2008

> Report of how the content of NDE's descriptions are influenced by the country and culture in which they took place.

Chapter Six: Winnowing – Shedding and Leaving Behind

Death and Dying vs. Life and Living

Kübler-Ross, E. On Death and Dying. Scribner, New York, 1969

> The modern classic that defined a genre. One of a handful of books I have ever read that I wish I had written. The inspiration for my memoir.

Erik Erikson

Erikson's theories of psychosocial development are summarized in two seminal volumes Childhood and Society, 1952 and Identity and the Life Cycle, 1953, both published by W. W. Norton, New York. In later years, Erikson, who worked well into his 90's, added a ninth stage of development as

described in The Life Cycle Complete, 1982, again published by
W. W. Norton.

Chapter Seven: Relapse

Bleeding to Death

Wysowski, D. et al. *Bleeding Complications with Warfarin Use: A
Prevalent Adverse Effect Resulting in Regulatory Action.* <u>JAMA
Archives of Internal Medicine</u>. 167:1414 -19, 2007

> A study of 29,000 Adverse Drug Events (ADE's)
> in Emergency Rooms in the US revealing that
> Warfarin/Coumadin account for 16% of ADE's
> and 33% for people over 50 years old.

Linkins, L. et al. *Clinical impact of bleeding in patients taking
oral anticoagulant therapy for venous thromboembolism: a
meta-analysis.* <u>Annals of Internal Medicine.</u> 139: 893 – 900,
2003

> Meta-analysis of 33 studies involving 4,373
> patients indicated that 1.3% to 7.2% per year on
> anticoagulants have a major bleed of which
> 13.4% end in death.

Carrier, M. et al. *Systematic review: case-fatality rates of
recurrent venous thromboembolism and major bleeding events
among patients treated for venous thromboembolism.* <u>Annals of
Internal Medicine</u>. 152:578 - 89, 2010 doi: 10.7326/0003-
4819-152-9-201005040-00008.

> Meta-analysis of 69 studies showed that .2% of
> patients have a major bleeding event in the first
> 3 months of anticoagulation therapy of which
> 11.3% are fatal.

ACKNOWLEDGEMENTS

While writing this book I was fortunate to have the support and assistance of many people. My three sisters helped enormously. Barrie for reading the manuscript as it was developing and providing comments and suggestions for improvement. Ellen for contributing her impressions and recollections of the days of crisis. Joanne for inadvertently providing the springboard for an interesting discussion on the power of prayer.

Others were equally instrumental shaping what became The Next Breath. Hank Weed, my friend of nearly three decades, reviewed the document in its formative stages and provided much needed input and support. My first wife, who prefers to remain anonymous, provided a valuable counter perspective that helped me to better understand my recovery journey. My best wishes for her continued ability to beat the odds.

As she has for many years, Cara Davis helped with research and production. Sandy Doubles and Debbie Norris also helped put the book together. My friend and creative resource extraordinaire Christopher Fous was the inspiration behind the book jacket and website:

www.the-next-breath.org

Despite how it might sound at the times in the pages of this book, I did receive quality care throughout this ordeal even though at the time I was often unable to recognize it as such. Thanks to Drs. Daniel Dosoretz, Stephen Hannan, Ashish Adi and Scott Dunbar for helping me through the crisis and Drs. Calvin Wei and Elizabeth Guardiani when I relapsed. Dr. Paul

Mantel and Dina Porter LPN have stood by me faithfully for my continued care when lesser caregivers would have abandoned me. I will be forever grateful to them.

Two additional people deserve special thanks. Linda Conklin lent a nonjudgmental ear when I needed one and offered insights and encouragement. Irv Feferman was my sympathetic and knowledgeable life line when I was floundering. Irv was kind enough to read the manuscript afterward as well.

Of course, if there are any errors in the text as there might well be with such a technical subject, I am solely responsible. The same can be said for any unevenness in presentation where I have given a topic less emphasis than it deserves or have omitted important stakeholders or organizations.

Mostly though, I want to thank my immediate family for making this work possible. Writing a book is an act of faith. You have to believe someone will want to hear what you have to say. Doubts abound. It is also a long and laborious process that takes away from other things. For the sacrifices they made and their undying love and support I thank my children Jake and Jane, always my closest friends, and my partner and wife of 35 years, Dorit, the love of my life and dedicate this book to them.

ABOUT THE AUTHOR

After a successful career in market research and public health policy consulting Joe Fisher now writes full time from his home base in Sanibel Island, Fl. His earlier work has received praise from *Publishers Weekly*, *The Miami Herald* and the *New England Journal of Medicine* among others.

With a doctorate in Sociology (Tufts University) and a Master of Public Health degree (Harvard University) Joe is well qualified to speak to the consequences of life-threatening medical emergencies from both a professional and personal perspective.

OTHER BOOKS BY THE AUTHOR

Killer Among Us: Public Reactions to Serial Murder

Advertising, Alcohol Consumption and Abuse:
A Worldwide Survey

Advertising, Alcohol Consumption and Mortality:
An Empirical Investigation

Made in the USA
Lexington, KY
15 February 2015